MANHATTANIZING™ LAS VEGAS

How to Profit from the
Second Phase of Vertical Growth

SECOND EDITION

To Kirby,

To creating synergies together,

Paul Murad

5/21/2009

Manhattanizing™ Las Vegas

How to Profit from the
Second Phase of Vertical Growth

Second Edition

Paul Murad

Lotus Press
New York

The Las Vegas real estate market is dynamic by nature. Therefore, it is likely that even at the time of publication, individual projects may have changed. It is also likely that newly announced or cancelled projects are not included in this book.

For up-to-date information on vertical developments and investment opportunities in Las Vegas, contact Paul Murad directly at paul@paulmurad.com or call his office at 702-450-2343. For more information visit www.ManhattanizingLasVegas.com.

MANHATTANIZING™ *Las Vegas*

Published by Lotus Press, New York

Cover art by Anthony Pangallo
Photography by Carlo Roncancio

First Edition: June 2005
Second Edition: December 2007

ISBN: 978-0-9769531-3-5

Printed in the United States of America

Table of Contents

Prologue
From Exuberance to Measured Growth

When I was transitioning from residential to commercial brokerage, I realized that there were many misconceptions about the Las Vegas market, and that there was not a comprehensive source of information for real estate professionals and the general public. At that point, I decided to write the first edition of *Manhattanizing™ Las Vegas: How to Profit from the Next Phase of Mega Growth*.

I spent hundreds of hours researching and conducting interviews with developers, government officials, construction companies, lenders, real estate professionals, and individual buyers and sellers of real estate to create a single source that provides an accurate representation of the market.

The success of the first book led to this second edition and will be followed by future editions. *Manhattanizing™ Las Vegas* has also helped pave the way for a Manhattanizing™ series of books that will chronicle real estate activity around the nation's most exciting cities.

Much has happened in the Las Vegas real estate market since I wrote the first edition early in 2005. No one anticipated how quickly the market would change. The vertical market in Las Vegas went from unbridled excitement to skepticism in a matter of months.

This rapid transition served as a catalyst for numerous inquiries from readers and, in turn, influenced my decision to write a second edition of *Manhattanizing™ Las Vegas*. This edition will help readers understand how the changes in the market affect investments and, in this context, update them on the status of current and future projects while discussing how to profit during this next phase of Manhattanization.

This edition provides much more than an overview of the vertical residential market in Las Vegas. It offers unique insights and knowledge about new developments that will prove invaluable to buyers, investors, real estate professionals, developers, and interested observers. Most importantly, readers will discover how to profit from this dynamic market.

Introduction

Manhattanizing Las Vegas

The term *Manhattanizing*, or *Manhattanization*, refers to the process by which cities begin growing vertically after decades of horizontal growth and urban sprawl. As cities begin reaching their physical and practical outward limits, people begin moving inward (toward city centers) and upward.

Manhattanizing also describes the revitalization of downtown areas when suburbs become inconvenient for residents faced with long commutes. Often, the term simply refers to building vertically (high-rise, mid-rise, or low-rise buildings) or converting older buildings for residential use, as occurred in New York City, Chicago, Miami, and other large, mature cities.

Although it is a frequently used buzzword, the term *Manhattanizing* may not be the most accurate way to describe what is happening in Las Vegas. The term does indeed describe the next stage of aggressive real estate development, but it may also refer to something that is *not* happening in Las Vegas.

Unlike Manhattan, which went vertical for industrial and business reasons, Las Vegas went vertical for entertainment reasons. Since there are few old warehouses or factories in Las Vegas to convert into residential units, developers must begin with unused or under-used land and build from the ground up.

Perhaps a more precise term for describing the vertical growth in Las Vegas is *Miamization.* Like Miami, Las Vegas is a tourist destination. Miami has its beaches with beach front property, and Las Vegas has the Strip with "Strip-front" property.

People from around the world who have the means and desire to purchase a vacation home in destinations such as South Beach or Las Vegas seek luxurious, hassle-free properties. Instead of spending money on hotel rooms, they prefer a property that they own and that they can furnish to their tastes. They also want access to shopping, dining, and entertainment.

They may also choose Miami or Las Vegas for tax reasons since neither Florida nor Nevada collects state income tax. Furthermore, Miami and Las Vegas both have major cities that feed them with tourists (New York for Miami, and Los Angeles for Las Vegas).

Each of these factors creates a demand for a certain type of housing product—luxury vertical residences.

In addition to second- and third-home buyers, the economies of Miami and Las Vegas draw new residents. While Miami continues to grow, Las Vegas has been and continues to be one of the fastest growing cities in the United States. New housing options are needed for incoming residents; however, land has become short in supply.

Investors in both Miami and Las Vegas have identified opportunities associated with dramatic growth and increased demand for housing. A lot of money was invested in the changing skyline of Miami, and we are seeing similar investments in Las Vegas properties.

Perhaps the most interesting similarity between Miami and Las Vegas is that developers in both cities find it easier to tear down existing buildings to make room for new developments. This is not the case in other major cities such as Manhattan or San Francisco.

In the words of Las Vegas City Manager Douglas A. Selby, when it comes to Manhattanizing Las Vegas, "developers have a clean slate. They had to build high-rises from scratch." This is more a characteristic of Miami than Manhattan.

Although it is imprecise, the term *Manhattanizing* has entered the Las Vegas lexicon. It is used by developers, the media, the general public, and the City's mayor to describe Las Vegas development. While we have yet to see if neighborhood stores, restaurants, delis, and dry-cleaners pop up around the new projects, we do know that Las Vegas is going vertical.

When I first began studying the investment opportunities offered by high-rise condominiums and other vertical residences, there were very few examples of them in Las Vegas. In 2005, few people in Las Vegas showed an interest in living in, much less investing in, a vertical property. Then suddenly, it seemed as if everyone was talking about vertical living.

Developers were becoming celebrities and celebrities were becoming developers.

In slightly over a year, nearly a hundred high-rise projects were announced in Las Vegas—not to mention dozens of mid- and low-rise projects. While it is true that many of the announced projects will not be built, the excitement did prove that there is a market for vertical living and that the option opens many opportunities for investment.

In the following pages, you will learn about the unique and profitable investment opportunities that accompany the next phase of development in Las Vegas. I will outline the projects that are currently being built or that are on the drawing board, and also share with you tips for investing in this type of property.

This book's purpose is to educate you on how to adapt to and capitalize on this new market, whether you are only beginning to consider investing, are new to investing in vertical properties, or are already an experienced investor.

As with any book about a dynamic market of this nature, the projects discussed in the following pages may change from the time I write these words to the time you read them. It is likely that new projects will be announced and some projects may fail. Regardless of such changes, the messages of this book will remain relevant to those interested in investing in the Manhattanizing of Las Vegas.

Chapter One
Market Overview

From Exuberance to Measured Growth

As I write this book, the media has focused on the gloomy side of Las Vegas's vertical development. I suppose it is more interesting to report on stormy weather than on another sunny day. While bad news is intriguing, intelligent buyers and investors look beyond stories of failure. They discern the reasons for failure and ways to capitalize on a market that continues to expand and deliver high returns on investment.

Of the more than a hundred announced high-rise projects, relatively few have failed. Yes, they were large and noticeable failures, but as with projects involving hundreds of millions of dollars in a competitive market, one should expect a few casualties. Those that survive will present investors with opportunities that were not available in the more glamorous days of unbridled excitement about vertical condominium developments in Las Vegas.

The truth is that the market elements that made the Las Vegas real estate market attractive to investors in the last boom continue to exist. For instance, Las Vegas continues to have high population growth month after month. While mortgage rates have risen from record lows and prices have risen to match rising construction costs, people still need housing. Aggressive investors seeking to make a quick $100,000 may not find the current environment attractive, but a more realistic market continues to offer many opportunities for serious investors. As in other maturing cities, longer-term investments are the future of Las Vegas real estate.

Understanding what led to the next phase of Manhattanization will help you invest intelligently and successfully in a fluctuating market. Those who are willing to commit to researching the available properties and market circumstances will be rewarded with post-boom opportunities.

Good News for Investors

The Las Vegas vertical construction boom began decades ago and will persist throughout the foreseeable future. The basic factors that made the Las Vegas real estate market attractive when the first boom began remain today. These factors involve the continual growth of the city and a shrinking supply of developable land. The population of Southern Nevada is expected to increase 53 percent from 2006 to 2024. At this rate, Las Vegas's population should reach 3 million people in less than two decades.

Why are people moving to Las Vegas in such large numbers? Certainly, the climate is a factor, as well as the lifestyle, but they are also moving to Las Vegas for economic reasons. Las Vegas continues to have one of the lowest unemployment rates in the country and the strongest job growth.

According to Dr. Keith Schwer, economist at the University of Nevada, Las Vegas, Clark County witnessed the creation of 45,000 new jobs in 2006. The median income is also expected to rise significantly with the job growth rate.

People also move to Las Vegas because of Nevada's lack of a state income tax. This advantage is particularly attractive to wealthy people who may only live in Las Vegas long enough to establish legal residence. They may then spend their time at houses in other states or countries. It is important to keep this population in mind when considering the vertical market, since luxury condominiums offer the convenience and amenities that second- and third-home buyers demand.

Globalization is also bringing people from around the world to Las Vegas. As people gain wealth in other countries, they often seek homes and real estate investments in the United States. They do this not only for the prestige of owning property in the U.S., but more importantly, they seek tangible assets in a country that is possibly more economically stable than their own.

The world's wealthy also choose to purchase homes in Las Vegas because of the international popularity of the city. As I travel the world (I have been to about 50 countries), I am always surprised by the interest people have in this medium-sized American city. They often ask me about real estate opportunities in Las Vegas before they inquire about New York, Miami, or Los Angles.

Many of Las Vegas's new residents need homes. As people pour into Las Vegas, developers respond by quickly building new residences. In an expanding market, developers have the luxury of pre-selling their homes before they are built. Unfortunately, this opportunity led to wild speculation during the last boom, and resulted in a market adjustment to return supply to the levels of demand.

The good and the bad news is that this situation has given investors a unique opportunity. Unlike people who are moving to Las Vegas for work, investors have the luxury of waiting for a residence to be built, which can take as long as two to three years.

Once the home is built, there are people who have an immediate need for a new home. These people are willing to pay the appreciated price for the home and move in right away.

While many people have profited by investing this way, the negative side of this strategy is higher real estate costs. As houses appreciated quickly throughout 2005, the effect was a slowing down the market for single-family homes.

The demand for homes throughout 2003 and 2005, when interest rates where relatively low and the stock market had an unimpressive record, Las Vegas real estate became a commodity not only for domestic investors, but for foreign investors as well.

Foreign investors capitalized on the weak U.S. dollar by purchasing real estate in America.

While it is true that interest rates are rising, they have not risen to levels that will permanently or significantly affect the real estate market, especially in a market like Las Vegas where demand continues to be high relative to other parts of the country.

To keep up with demand, new tracks of land need to be developed. The current rate of land absorption in the Las Vegas Valley is around 5,500 acres per year. At this rate, we can expect to run out of land by 2017.

When people look at Southern Nevada they question why Las Vegas is running out of land. One would assume that the city could continue to expand in the same manner as Phoenix, but this is not the case. It is true that, unlike Phoenix, Las Vegas is surrounded by mountains, but the lack of land involves more than mountains.

Most of Nevada is owned by the federal government. Besides the military installations north of Las Vegas, the Bureau of Land Management (BLM) manages most of the other federally-owned land throughout Nevada.

When Las Vegas began expanding, the federal government established a boundary for the expansion. At the time of this writing, there are less than 65,000 acres left that can be released for development. It would take an act of Congress and the signature of the President to extend the boundary for development.

Passing such a measure would be a long and difficult task. There are wildlife and land conservation issues that would have to be addressed, such as the impact of development on endangered species like the desert tortoise. Also, people concerned about sprawl cite the stress that growth imposes on natural resources, such as the very real concern about the county's water supply. Many conservationists and other concerned people would object to any act of Congress that would make more land available for development in Southern Nevada.

As we approach this outer limit of available land, not only is land becoming increasingly expensive, but the available parcels are also becoming less attractive for development. True, there remain some great sites throughout the city and along the outer edges of the city, but developers must now look for sites that, for various reasons, have remained vacant for decades as the city grew around them and past them.

The only solution to the land shortage, short of an act of Congress to release more land, is to build upward, stacking residences upon a single parcel of land. Such a strategy not only deals with the shortage of land in the Las Vegas Valley, but also with environmental concerns. Vertical residences use fewer natural resources than traditional single-family homes.

However, the demand for high-density living involves more than land shortages, resource usage, and economics; there is also a real demand for vertical housing.

A new urban class is moving to Las Vegas from large cities such as New York, Miami, Chicago, San Francisco, and San Diego. These new residents demand the convenience and amenities that vertical living delivers. They are not interested in acquiring homes far out in the suburbs with long commutes and yards that need tending; instead, they wish to live near where they work and play.

The demographic that is interested in living in low-maintenance condominiums is expected to double in the coming years for a few reasons. First, fewer couples are choosing to have children. Referred to as "DINKs" (Double Income, No Kids), these people not only dedicate themselves to work and recreation, but they also seek to live in trouble-free communities near entertainment options.

Second, more Americans are choosing to live alone. Their numbers are expected to rise from 7.5 million to 10 million by 2013. These people do not want large homes with small yards in the suburbs. Instead, they seek the comforts of smaller homes close to amenities and entertainment venues.

Third, a demographic known as Echo Boomers is approaching the age of 25 now, at a rate of 4 million people per year. Echo Boomers may not have the income required to purchase expensive properties, but they are seeking options for their first homes.

Lastly, perhaps the most important demographic for the high-density housing market is the Baby Boomers. Once their children leave home, Baby Boomers find the lifestyle of vertical living more to their liking. Baby Boomers and retirees tend to enjoy properties that have minimal upkeep so they can focus on travel and other priorities.

Over the next decade, there will be an expected rise of 25 percent in the number of people over the age of 50 in the United States. This group will have more money than any previous generation because of inheritances, dual incomes and rising real estate values. Whether residency is full-time or part-time, we can expect many people in the 50-plus age range to choose Las Vegas as a place to purchase a home.

According to the National Association of Realtors, 36 percent of homes sold in 2006 were bought as second homes. This number includes investment properties as well as vacation homes.

Surprising for many is the fact that most people who buy second homes are in the middle class, earning less than $100,000 a year. The main reason is that real estate is a more solid and understandable investment than other alternatives. It is also true that people are more mobile these days, making the need for a second home—even if it is just a vacation home—more common.

While there are certainly middle-income investors in the Las Vegas market, Las Vegas is one of the most popular sites on the planet where the truly wealthy come to play. These people prefer the convenience of owning a vertical residence in close proximity to the entertainment on the Strip.

Frequent visitors may also find it more convenient and less costly to purchase a condominium on or near the Strip than to stay in resort casinos. In the past, casinos discounted and comped rooms to "high-roller" gamblers; however, since room rates have risen, casinos are reluctant to comp their more expensive rooms. As rooms become expensive and less available to frequent visitors, many visitors seek a more permanent lodging option.

New high-rise condominium products, known as condo-hotels, are beginning to catch the eye of the frequent Las Vegas visitors. These condominiums act as hotel suites when the owners are not using them.

With 39.1 million visitors in 2006, Las Vegas has an increasing demand for hotel rooms. Condo-hotels allow people to generate cash flow on their property when they are not using it. Even better, they allow investors to get involved in a market that was once reserved for large hotels (See Chapter 6 for a more detailed discussion of condo-hotels).

All of these factors—land shortage, changes in demographics, increasing population, and the second-home market—combine to create a demand for vertical residences in Las Vegas.

At this point, supply is behind demand. It takes years to plan and build a high-rise condominium. Moreover, when several large companies focus on completing multibillion-dollar structures, they absorb a significant amount of the contractors and laborers. This situation will delay and complicate the completion of other projects because labor/contractors respond to higher paying projects. Therefore, small condominium projects are postponed. The result is that vertical residences—especially more affordable options—are on par with demand.

All of this is good news for investors and buyers. It means that there is a strong likelihood that a property purchased today will appreciate in the long run, and deliver a good return on your investment.

Do not allow negative stories about high-rise condominiums in Las Vegas to cloud your understanding of the market's demand for vertical living and the opportunity for investment.

Bad News for Developers (And Good News for Investors)

Even with the high demand for vertical residences, developers have recently faced tough times. The first source of their troubles was skyrocketing construction costs. For instance, the price of concrete escalated significantly in 2003 and it continues to rise as worldwide demand for concrete causes shortages.

Other material costs have also increased; for instance, gypsum, the main component of drywall, has risen 42 percent from 2005 to 2006. Worse, there have been general shortages of drywall throughout the world. Also, the price of copper, which is used in wiring, pipes, and fixtures, increased 70 percent in two years. From November 2005 to May 2006, the price of 24-gauge wiring used to wire buildings jumped from $3.15 to $5.75 per pound.

Furthermore, as all of us are aware, the cost of fuel has increased dramatically and continues to rise. The cost of diesel fuel used in transportation and construction equipment rose 36 cents per gallon in one year. With as much diesel as the cranes and heavy equipment use on a job site, this increase has a serious impact on the bottom line. Increases in petroleum prices also cause price increases in plastic products such as PVC pipes and roofing materials.

These price increases have changed how subcontractors bid on a project. In the past, bids for electrician subcontractors, for example, were good for 30 days. Nowadays, bids are only good for 24 to 48 hours. For a major project, those time frames mean significant fluctuations in construction cost estimates.

The costs continued to increase through 2007. This means that if a developer determined pricing based on construction costs in early 2004, and pre-sold the property based on those calculations, in 2007 the developer would realize a loss of profits and in some cases would not be able to complete the building based on the prices paid for the units. If a developer is going to lose money on a project, one shouldn't be surprised when the project is cancelled.

While these cost increases have hurt developers and have caused projects to be cancelled, they have had little impact on demand and on the potential return on investment that early buyers received. In fact, in a multiple tower project, the people purchasing in the first phase saw dramatic appreciation as the developer raised prices in future phases to compensate for escalating construction costs.

Equally challenging for developers is the shortage of qualified skilled labor in Las Vegas. When developers became aware of the demand for vertical living, many of them rushed to the market without considering how they were going to build their projects. They assumed they would easily find contractors and sub-contractors. Unfortunately, with so many vertical projects appearing simultaneously, there is a shortage of qualified construction workers and equipment operators.

Once demand for construction companies rose, contractors and sub-contractors began charging more for their labor. They could also afford to be selective on which projects they would work.

This situation was amplified when large companies such as MGM Mirage began building billion-dollar projects. These large companies have the autonomy, resources, and economies of scale to pay more than the market price to attract construction workers to their projects. The construction companies themselves are not only attracted to the money, but they also prefer the stability of working for larger, more established companies.

MGM Mirage's $7.8 billion CityCenter is expected to employ up to 7,000 construction workers at its peak construction activity; that is nearly a third of Southern Nevada's total union trade workforce.

Other billion-dollar construction projects are also draining the labor pool; these include Trump Towers,

Steve Wynn's Encore, and the Venetian's Palazzo expansion. The $4.4 billion Echelon Place by Boyd Gaming will also use a significant percentage of the Southern Nevada workforce.

Faced with all of these factors, several vertical projects were put on hold and others were cancelled.

Cancelled or Suspended Projects

Allure – Tower 2	Liberty Tower
Aqua Blue	Majestic
Cielo Vista	Opus
Club Renaissance	Red Rock Residences
Curve	Sandhurst
Hard Rock Residences	SpaLofts
Icon	Spanish View Towers
Ivana	Urban Village
Krystle Sands	Vegas 888
Las Ramblas	W Hotel Residences

However, from the investor's perspective, the struggles developers face are not always a negative. For instance, the labor shortage is not a bad thing for investors. First of all, it means a lot of people living in Las Vegas will be making more money and be able to afford better housing.

Also, as the demand and pay for construction workers increases, people from other parts of the country are likely to come to Las Vegas for work. These people may not settle permanently in Las Vegas; instead, they may opt to rent until they are finished with a construction project.

In both scenarios, the demand for housing increases dramatically at the same time that production has slowed. The people coming to Las Vegas do not have the luxury of buying at pre-construction prices because they need a home immediately. They will have to buy or rent existing homes.

As you can see, the bad news for developers should have minimal impact on investors. In fact, the situation should provide the smart investor with opportunities. The vertical market in Las Vegas is nowhere near doomed. We have only switched from a period of exuberance to an era of experience and expertise.

Other Differences to Consider in the Las Vegas Market

The Las Vegas vertical market is often unjustly compared with other cities. New York City, Miami, Chicago, and San Diego are all much larger cities than Las Vegas, with diverse markets with large corporate headquarters.

Las Vegas's market is becoming increasingly diverse, but it is still relatively limited. Besides the gaming industry, Las Vegas hosts few major company headquarters. Other major cities have matured after years industrial and commercial development. They have had years of urban infill and years of high-rise development. By comparison, Las Vegas is a toddler.

Take Miami for instance: Turnberry Associates greatly contributed to the launch of the luxury condominium concept in Florida in the 1950s. Soon after, they were joined by other large developers, such as WSG Development, Ian Bruce Eichner, Swire, WCI Communities, and the Related Group.

As Douglas E. Lein of DEL Consulting points out, these other cities have a stable and well-capitalized developer base. They have market data available so lenders are able to perform due diligence for underwriting. The developers are also familiar with the contractors in the area and are better able to predict costs.

Las Vegas is a much younger city. High-rise condominium development is only now beginning and the infrastructures that support vertical housing are just now being put into place. After only 48 months of urban infill and few projects completed, there is still little real-time and comparable data available on the Las Vegas vertical-housing market. Without industry studies, banks and lenders are reluctant to invest in high-cost vertical projects.

As a result, developers have had to rely on speculative investment, which is not only more expensive, but also requires higher profit margins to be considered successful. Also, more of a building must be pre-sold before funds will be released to begin construction.

To reach these higher margins, many marketers have been overly aggressive in their efforts to draw attention to their projects. Prices of units were set long before a general contractor was selected. This meant sales and marketing companies were making decisions based on assumed prices per square foot without calculating the increase in construction costs. Marketing companies pre-sold several projects that were priced too low. Consequently, once projects began to take shape, developers could not compensate for the increase in costs.

Many developers found it easier to simply cancel projects than to continue with such low profit margins. According to Doug Lein, "no project failed for lack of absorption." Demand remained strong for the projects and buyers were willing to pay prices the developers set. Unfortunately, not all developers did enough due diligence to survive the realities of the market.

These aggressive marketing tactics assisted in the over-dramatizing of project failures. Advertising campaigns successfully attracted buyers, and they made the general public aware of potential projects. Later, when the projects were cancelled, everyone took notice. Thus the marketing companies, as well as the media, tended to over-dramatize the cancellations, causing the public to perceive a greater percentage of cancellations than really existed.

A similar situation occurred in the 1990s in South Florida. There was a lot of exuberance and hype surrounding the real estate market prior to the 1990s. Developers rushed to sell new buildings and investors were quick to invest. When there were failures and some projects were not built, many people predicted the end of the high-rise condominium market. However, a decade later, the market was as strong as ever. In reality, those few years of correction were a good opportunity for forward-thinking investors who understood the general trends and analyzed the reasons behind the failures.

While there is negative press today about the failure of high-profile projects, the lessons of South Florida teach us that vertical residences will continue to be built. The factors that made them attractive a couple years ago are still with us today. People are streaming into Las Vegas, and developable land is running out. Land prices are rising, and lot sizes are shrinking. Everything points to the need for high-density vertical housing.

As we look to the future, it is amazing how soon Las Vegas will look more like the major cities throughout the world. With an increasingly jagged skyline, the development of vibrant urban communities, and the creation of beautiful Strip-front properties, we are truly witnessing the Manhattanizing of Las Vegas.

Chapter Two
The Strip

Las Vegas Valley CONDO MAP

The Strip

Existing

01 Regency Towers
02 Park Towers
03 Turnberry Place
04 Turnberry Towers
05 Metropolis
06 Sky Las Vegas
07 Allure – Tower 1
08 The Signature at MGM Grand
09 Platinum
10 Panorama – Towers 1 & 2

Under Construction

11 Panorama – Tower 3
12 Onyx
13 Trump International
14 Palms Place
15 CityCenter
16 Cosmopolitan

Cancelled

17 Aqua Blue
18 Icon
19 Krystle Sands
20 Vegas 888
21 Las Ramblas
22 Hard Rock Residences
23 Majestic
24 Allure – Tower 2

Map Area:

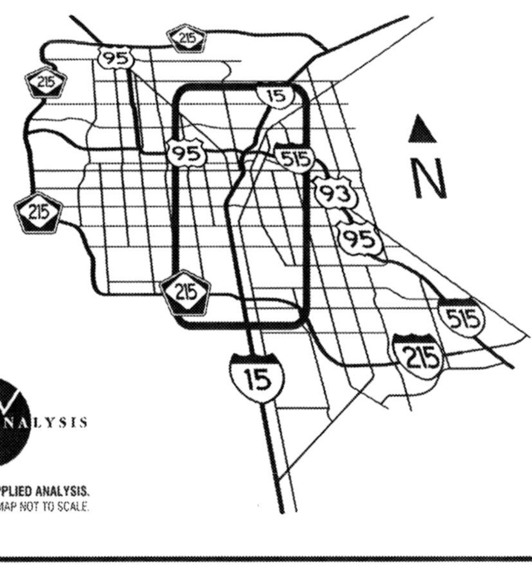

Las Vegas Valley CONDO MAP

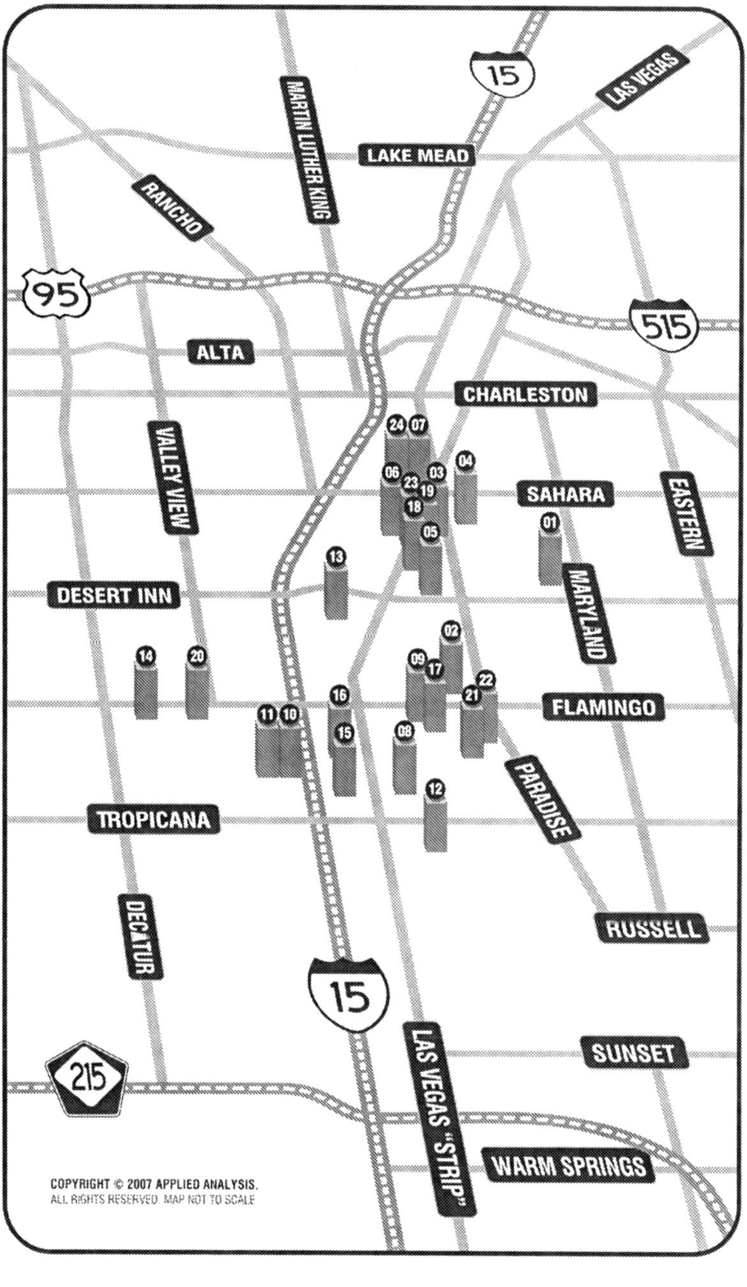

Las Vegas' Beach

The Strip is *the* major tourist attraction for Las Vegas. Developers refer to it as Las Vegas's ocean. Just as high-rises line the world's famous beaches, soon high-rise condominiums will loop around the Strip. These "Strip-front" residences are among the most impressive condominiums Las Vegas offers.

Many people, especially the world's wealthy, want to own a residence that is close to all the Strip has to offer. Since location is a major determinant of price, those located on or near the Strip command some of the highest prices in Southern Nevada.

An investor interested in property along the Strip should realize that while there are people worldwide who are interested in buying a vacation home along the Strip, the population that can afford a million-dollar second home is relatively limited. However, when we study the high-rise market in other destination cities such as Miami we see a substantial demand for luxury products.

Most of the available projects on or near the Strip are associated with casinos. These properties are usually condo-hotels (discussed in Chapter 6). Condo-hotels offer ownership along the Strip while adding to the room count of the casinos. For a variety of reasons, condo-hotels are attractive to second-home buyers and investors.

In this chapter, I discuss the more traditional condominium projects along or near the Strip.

Regency Towers

While vertical living in Las Vegas has only recently increased in popularity, it had its very beginnings in the 1970s with the construction of several apartment and condominium towers. One of the most well known is the Regency Towers, built in 1974.

This 28-story, 218-unit structure has housed many famous people throughout the years: Debbie Reynolds, Rodney Dangerfield, and LaToya Jackson. Recently, younger professionals have taken an interest in Regency Towers, buying up units as they become available.

Regency Towers has views across the Las Vegas Country Club toward the Strip and the Wynn Casino. While the building is older than other vertical residences currently available, Regency Towers has the feel of vintage condominiums in Miami, Chicago, and New York. The construction quality, floor plans, and central location contribute to its lasting value.

Hint: *Because Regency Towers is older than other properties, some units may need a lot of fixing up.*

These units are usually priced better and can increase value significantly with a little elbow grease.

Park Towers

Despite his reputation as an innovator and risk-taker, Irwin Molasky was actually conservative when he built Park Towers. He built relatively few units and kept construction height low compared to nearby structures such as casinos and office buildings. Now that we have seen the success of other projects and the number of new projects rising above the horizon, we may admire Molasky's initial conservative approach to the Park Towers project.

It took Molasky four years to sell 84 units; compare this to today's market, where the same number of units could sell in a matter of months.

Park Towers consists of two towers, each with 84 units. With prices ranging from $1.4 to $5 million, and floor plans between 2,100 and 5,550 square feet, the Park Towers were designed for a niche clientele. As its marketing materials said, Park Towers was designed for people whose "caviar has to be Beluga, the crystal no less than Baccarat, the champagne nothing but Dom Perignon or Cristal."

Yet behind Wynn and Molasky's confidence that Park Towers would become the "best residential building in the country," there existed a sense of unease. Concerning his project, Molasky once said, "It's a giant leap of faith,"

Who wouldn't be uneasy about constructing a $124 million building in an untested market? At the time, there was no sense of a huge demand for luxury high-rise living in Las Vegas. Molasky believed there were a limited number of people interested in high-end, high-rise housing, but proved himself wrong.

As it turns out, there are plenty with the means and desire to purchase a unit in a luxury project. Molasky now believes that the future of Las Vegas is in vertical living. However, he does not believe that there will be many more projects that will match the price and luxury of Park Towers.

Hint: *The exclusive Park Towers is not only close to the Strip, but close to the growing Howard Hughes Center. As the Howard Hughes Center becomes a larger business hub, demand for the units at Park Towers will increase.*

Turnberry Place

While Molasky deserves credit for conceiving Park Towers before 1998, the truth is that Turnberry Place broke ground before Park Towers did. Where Molasky was conservative in his approach to luxury high-rise condos, Turnberry Associates from South Florida planned for a larger demand. Not only did Turnberry cost less per square foot than Park Towers, they also created additional amenities such as the $45 million Stirling Club, which offers dining, entertainment, and spa services to Turnberry residents as well as to non-resident club members.

Turnberry Associates has decades of experience developing residential and commercial properties, including more than 5,000 luxury condominiums and apartments, and 1,640 resort and hotel rooms. Turnberry Associates was founded in 1967 by Donald Soffer, who transformed a swamp in North Dade County, Florida into a planned community. This community became the city of Aventura, a prestigious Florida address.

Turnberry Associates recognized similarities between Las Vegas today and Miami in the 1990s. Both cities are international resort destinations with amenities that attract people from around the world. Just as demand for upscale condominiums grew decades ago in Miami, Turnberry Associates was able to predict that Las Vegas would develop a similar demand. And the developers at Turnberry were correct.

Perhaps their success in other parts of the country and their tactic of approaching the Las Vegas market from the outside led Turnberry Associates to correctly predict that there would not only be a market for luxury high-rise condominiums in Las Vegas, but a significant demand as well.

Turnberry began as a $650 million luxury high-rise project behind the failed El Rancho casino. Units ranged in size from 1,540 to 11,000 square feet and were priced from $450,000 to $4.5 million.

People from around the world quickly bought up available units long before Turnberry's four towers were built. This demand allowed Turnberry Associates to complete construction of all four towers two years ahead of schedule.

Founder Donald Soffer notes that Turnberry Place was something Las Vegas needed: "Vegas has become a very cosmopolitan city," he said. "There's great entertainment and arts; the restaurants are as good as any place in the world. You've got so many choices in Vegas. It's just a fun city."

Turnberry was developed with the understanding that discerning buyers would pay top dollar to live near the Las Vegas Strip. Bruce Weiner, President of Turnberry Pavilion Partners, said, "In most major cities, you see a time in development where people stop running into the suburbs and start coming back into the city. Then with time, a product like we've got seems to be in order."

Las Vegas has many wealthy jet-setters from around the world interested in living near the Strip. This means that in addition to the usual "infill" from the suburbs, people from outside the city also have an interest in buying a vertical residence in the concentrated corridors of Las Vegas. The unfortunate result of this demand is a product that is often too costly for most Las Vegas residents.

While Turnberry Place sold all its units some time ago, they continue to offer resale services. They have an on-site resale team that specializes in Turnberry Place properties, so that instead of having buyers wait years for a property to become available, the resale program offers properties that are available immediately. Many of the properties are already furnished for second-home buyers.

Hint: *In the fourth tower there are some smaller units that usually go for a better price per square foot compared to other, newer projects. Despite the size of the units, residents have access to all of the amenities and benefits of the location, making these smaller units hot commodities.*

Turnberry Towers

Luxury condominiums serve a specific market niche, but the real story of Las Vegas's vertical development includes more than luxury products. Turnberry Associates planned years ago, when they were still in the process of building Turnberry Place, to construct a more moderately priced high-rise development a couple blocks away called Turnberry Towers. At the time, this project was named Madison Towers; however, it was renamed Turnberry Towers to leverage the well-established name and brand that Turnberry Associates has created.

The goal of creating a more moderately priced high-rise development was thwarted by the hot market in the mid-2000's and rising construction costs. To deal with these market forces, Turnberry Towers ended up selling at much higher prices than the original units at Turnberry Place.

While not as luxurious as Turnberry Place, Turnberry Towers offers many amenities, including valet service, a fitness center with tennis courts, and an outdoor pool. Residents also have access to the Stirling Club at Turnberry Place.

The two 45-story towers consist of 600 units, ranging from 915 to 1,937 square feet. These units are priced from $500,000 to $1.3 million.

John Riordan, vice president of sales at Turnberry Associates, says "more people are considering purchasing a high-rise home today because of the privacy, location, amenities and lifestyle." This, he says, is the reason for Turnberry Towers' success.

Hint: *Turnberry Towers is close to the redevelopment of the north end of the Strip, including the multi-billion-dollar Echelon Place, MGM's CityCenter North project, the Fontainebleau Resort, and the Crown Las Vegas project on the site of the former Wet n' Wild water park. As this section of the Strip reinvents itself, the units in Turnberry Towers will increase in value. Buying a unit before the north end of the Strip fully develops is a good long-term investment.*

Metropolis

Following in the tradition of Park Towers and Turnberry, Metropolis was also designed for the more discerning resident, bringing something new to the high-end high-rise market: loft-style design.

Metropolis was built on the site of a failed timeshare project, blocks away from the Strip on the backside of the Wynn Resort golf course. Named for the city in the Superman comics, the Metropolis lofts have 19.5-foot-tall ceilings and views of the Strip. Units are from 844 to 5,342 square feet in size and range from $900,000 to $3 million.

After years of experience in building loft-style condominiums in Houston, Randall Davis came to Las Vegas to build this $40 million 20-story art-deco project. Davis introduced loft living to Houston and is credited with revitalizing Houston's downtown.

After a delay of about a year, all but three of the 71 units were sold when they broke ground in the summer of 2004. Despite this early success, Davis worried that the luxury condo market would become overcrowded. He saw a need for more moderately priced condominium products.

Metropolis opened in early 2006, attracting many young professionals. Unfortunately, the spire that was supposed to be built on the top of the building was cancelled because of the rising costs of building materials. Also missing from the project is the promised pool as well as landscaping around the front entry.

Hint: *The extremely tall windows face Wynn's golf course, so there will remain unobstructed views of the Strip for years to come. This will keep values of Metropolis units rising as more views become impaired by new projects.*

Panorama

The story of Panorama began with Laurence Hallier looking for a place to live in Las Vegas. He wanted a "cool" high-rise condominium, like those found in Miami, Seattle, and other major cities. He felt Turnberry Place was too stuffy for his taste, and Park Towers was too expensive.

Instead, Hallier decided to build his own condominium—a place where he and his friends would want to live. The result is a successful project that continues to draw the attention of the press as new Hollywood stars purchase residences in Panorama Towers.

Hallier can thank his partnership with Andrew Sasson, who runs a successful nightclub company, The Light Group, for the attention Panorama has received in Hollywood and around the world. Sasson's nightclubs have provided him with prestigious contacts, including celebrities and other wealthy individuals from around the world; from these contacts, he built an impressive database of prospective buyers.

The Panorama project was one of the first major high-rise projects, emerging shortly after the success of Turnberry Place. The original plan was to build two towers, but demand was so high that they have begun construction on a third tower and have plans for a fourth tower.

I think Panorama did it the right way by not overselling during the pre-sales stage. As one tower was completed, the construction crews moved to the site of the next tower. By contrast, many other developers market and try to pre-sell the entire project before construction begins.

Panorama is located across from the Bellagio Hotel, on the west side of Interstate 15. The architect firm Klai Juba and Associates—the name behind such renowned projects as Mandalay Bay, Luxor, Four Seasons, and Caesar's Palace—designed the first tower with a unique architectural opening in the center of the building on the twenty-second floor. Hollywood designer Graft is also involved in this project, which had unit prices originally ranging from $400,000 through $750,000, and penthouses up to $2 million.

Most of the initial buyers in Panorama Towers were second- and third-home buyers. Two-thirds of the buyers were from California. Hallier says Las Vegas is following the "Miami trend" of New Yorkers flying south for their second homes and vacation properties. He believes Las Vegas will be the Miami for major West Coast cities like Los Angeles, San Diego, and San Francisco.

Hallier believes that local residents will also take an interest in high-rise living in Las Vegas; as Las Vegas becomes a major city, more people will choose to live closer to the city's core to avoid long commutes.

Hallier and Sasson realize the need for retail support of high-rise buildings in Las Vegas. Their project will include a gourmet grocery by Chef Kerry Simon, Elizabeth Blau, and MGM Executive Chef Kim Canteenwalla; a European laundry and dry-cleaning store; and a bakery and coffeehouse. This retail center should open in front of the first tower in early 2008.

The units in the first tower originally sold for about $450 per square foot. Because of increases in construction prices, units in the third tower were selling at $600 per square foot. This has meant significant appreciation for the original buyers of the first units.

Hint: *Despite rising construction costs, the area on the west side of Interstate 15, across from the Strip, promises to be a "condo row." Other developers are making plans to follow suit. When the Harmon Avenue overpass opens, it will provide direct access to Project CityCenter and the Strip. Look to buy units before the Harmon Bridge and Project CityCenter projects are complete.*

Sky Las Vegas

Sky Las Vegas, the 45-story luxury high-rise condominium, towers over the Strip. Developers boast that when construction began on the $325 million project, not only were 80 percent of the units already sold, but a full two-thirds of those units were sold to residents rather than investors. The project was so successful that the original design of 40 floors was modified to include five additional floors.

Sky Las Vegas stands on the Strip just north of the Circus Circus Hotel and Casino. Units range in size from 870 to 5,500 square feet at costs ranging from $500,000 to $5 million. There are also three-story suites available that have rooftop garden patios.

The building itself, also designed by Klai Juba, is a contemporary design, featuring a sleek exterior of blue glass. The interiors were designed by Desjardins Design Group, the same Miami company that works with Turnberry Associates.

Hint: *Sky Las Vegas is the first condominium to open directly on the Strip. Because of this, Sky Las Vegas has been an extremely successful project. However, some buyers got in over their heads and are looking to unload their property. When this is the case, there is an opportunity to obtain a unit for significantly less than the asking price. Submit a low offer and see if they bite.*

Allure

When Chicago developer Fifield Company began clearing the site for Allure condominiums, more than 70 percent of the building had been reserved. Allure is a 41-story tower with 428 units that originally ranged in price from $550,000 to more than $4 million, and in size from 671 to 4,400 square feet.

While officially part of downtown Las Vegas, most people consider everything south of the Stratosphere part of the Las Vegas Strip. Allure stands on West Sahara Avenue, just steps away from the Strip. Residents have easy access to Interstate 15 while enjoying views of the Strip and downtown through 10-foot floor-to-ceiling windows.

Fifield Company is a 28-year-old company. It has built 40 high-rise towers in Chicago and at any given time has five to seven projects in development. Founder and CEO Steven Fifield has a unique view on the Las Vegas high-rise market; he says that recent high-profile project cancellations are a sign of a strong and aggressive market, not a weakness in demand. In fact, he says, "Demand is high, but there are limited resources and contractors. Only strong developers with a good record of accomplishment will be able to compete in this strong market."

There were plans to build another tower on the five-acre site next to the first tower, which was supposed to have as many as 400 units and cost anywhere from $300 million to $400 million to construct. However, the plans for the second condominium tower have been cancelled, and the current owner of the property is looking at building a casino and hotel tower, or to sell the property.

Hint: *As of this writing, the Fifield Company is still offering good pricing on units at Allure. Developers usually give great incentives during the final stretch of construction. Investigate what the developers are offering and then look at the resale units.*

Onyx

Before most people had even heard of the project, Onyx was sold out. The project itself appears to be on the fast track for completion with a 12-month construction schedule. It is expected to be completed by the end of 2007.

This low-rise project is located on Duke Ellington Way at Tropicana, behind the Hooters Casino. It is a four-story building with 63 units ranging in size from 740 to 2,300 square feet. The amenities consist of what one would expect from a condominium project this close to the Strip, including concierge services, a fitness center, and state-of-the-art pool. The townhome-style condos were priced from $450,000 to $950,000.

Hint: *From an investment standpoint, it is better to select a property that others will want to live in, not just one that you personally like. If you managed to get a unit at Onyx before it sold out, it will be viable for resale once the project is completed. When properties are selling out quickly, investigate why: are there people planning to live in their units, or are there only investors hoping that people will be attracted to the property? The more buyers planning to be residents, the better the resale opportunities will be.*

Chapter Three
Downtown

Las Vegas Valley **CONDO MAP**

Downtown

Existing

25 SoHo Lofts
26 Newport Lofts

Under Construction

27 Streamline Tower
28 Juhl

Pre-selling

29 Stanhi
30 Verge

Planned/Proposed

31 Union Park
32 Charlie Palmer Condo-Hotel
33 Gateway Las Vegas

Suspended

34 Evolution Lofts
35 HUE Lofts
36 Cielo Vista

Cancelled

37 Sandhurst
38 Ivana
39 Club Renaissance

Map Area:

APPLIED ANALYSIS

Las Vegas Valley CONDO MAP

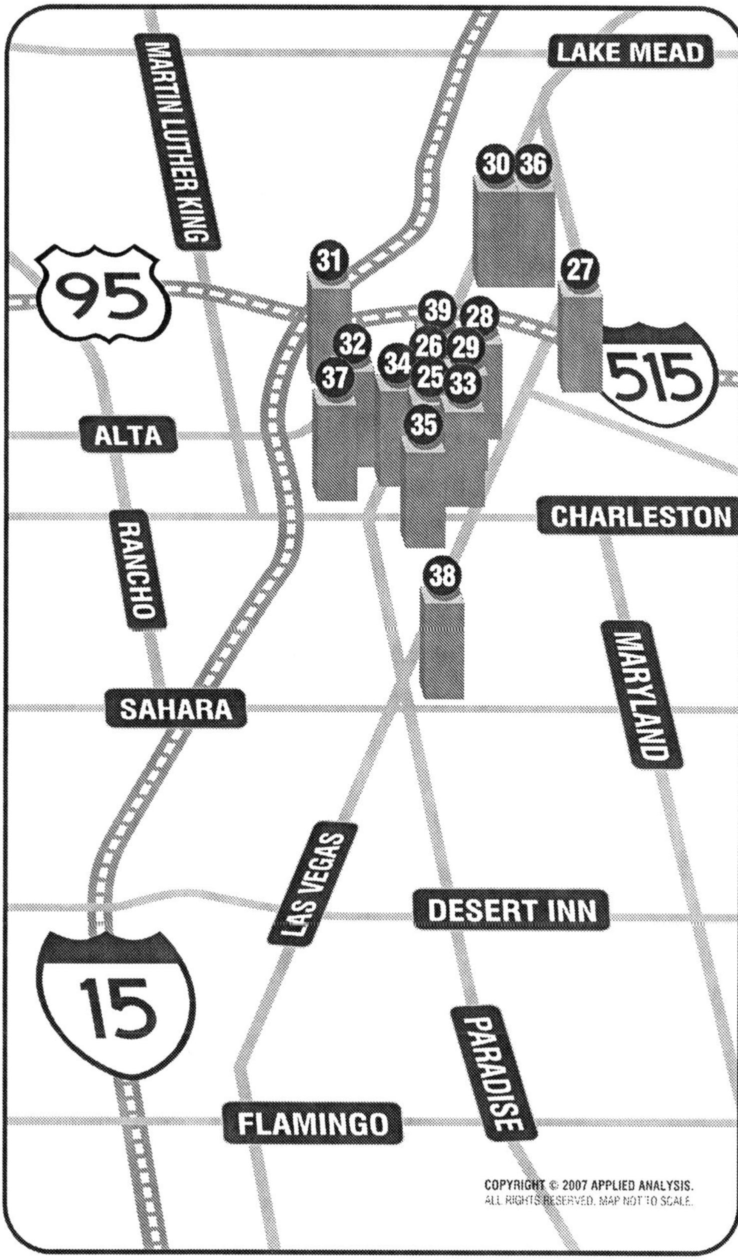

The Changing Core of Las Vegas

"Like it or not, downtown is the core of our city, the heart and soul of Southern Nevada, and without a healthy inner core, the city will rot from the inside out."
–Oscar Goodman

People have been curious about the fate of downtown Las Vegas. Many plans have been drawn, and as it turns out, its future does not belong exclusively to new casino development, but rather to a variety of different industries. The downtown area is quickly becoming a Mecca for an increasing number of non-gaming industries.

The World Market Center opened in July 2005 and was an instant success—so much so that construction began on the second building shortly after the first was completed. The World Market Center brings buyers for the furniture industry from around the world to visit Las Vegas to conduct business.

The first building is ten stories high with a staggering 1.3 million square feet of space. Skeptics were surprised when the entire building was leased before the concrete was dry.

The second building, with 1.6 million square feet of space, was completed in January of 2007.

Soon afterward, construction started on a third building, whose space was already leased before it broke ground. The building was topped off in October 2007.

When all the buildings are completed, they will provide 12 million square feet of space in eight buildings on 57 acres. In the first year it was open for business, the World Market Center contributed $1.3 billion to the Las Vegas economy.

The Chelsea Outlet Mall, located next to the World Market Center, also exceeded expectations, becoming one of the most successful outlet malls in the country. Parking quickly became an issue, so the mall built new parking garages to allow for expansion.

In the same area, the City of Las Vegas will have two new projects: the $50 million Lou Ruvo Alzheimer's Institute and the $150 million Fred W. and Mary B. Smith Center for the Performing Arts.

Besides drawing tourists to the downtown area, these enterprises provide employment for tens of thousands of people, all of whom will have to commute great distances unless adequate housing is available nearby. City officials and developers have seen a need to provide housing options for these workers within the downtown area.

There are many positive indicators suggesting that development will continue to occur downtown, and developers are continually showing an interest in the area. As Scott Adams of the Office of Business Development for the City of Las Vegas puts it, "downtown is where the big players can do what they are good at."

Douglas E. Lein of DEL Consulting says, "If you offer the option, people will buy close to work." He believes that there could be 6,000 to 8,000 residential units in downtown Las Vegas by 2013. He praises the City of Las Vegas for allowing the private sector to decide what the market will support.

The City of Las Vegas has gone to great lengths to encourage development downtown. Supportive and forward-thinking City officials have lifted many building restrictions found in other parts of the Las Vegas Valley. They have also accommodated developers in other ways, such as allowing them to set up staging areas and closing lanes and roads during construction.

The City's ultimate goal is to create a pedestrian-friendly downtown where retail, dining, and entertainment amenities are all within walking distance of offices and residences. In fact, the City requires that the ground floor of all high-rise projects consist of retail space. This means that soon residents will be able to live in downtown Las Vegas with little need for their car, much like the downtowns of other major cities.

The people who have trouble seeing this vision of downtown usually cannot overlook the presence of run-down neighborhoods and buildings. However, the City of Las Vegas is actively working with businesses and landlords to improve the look of downtown.

Dr. Douglas Selby, City Manager of the City of Las Vegas, says, "As prices go up, poor neighborhoods will convert into other, newer projects." He points to the effect Allure has had on surrounding land prices. The area around Allure was once in distress, but now prices are rising quickly and property owners have an incentive to improve their properties or to sell them to businesses interested in catering to the residents of Allure.

In a few short years, the look and feel of downtown Las Vegas will be very different from what we see now. Investors need to realize and anticipate this change, as there will be many new opportunities when people and businesses move downtown.

Union Park

More than a hundred years ago, William Clark founded Las Vegas to support his railroad. Now, the last major land holdings of the Union Pacific Railroad are becoming the epicenter for redevelopment, referred to as Union Park or the 61 Acres.

In place of the old stockyards, by 2012 Union Park will be filled with high-, mid-, and low-rise buildings, an arts district, a medical research hospital, and various parks. Las Vegas has certainly come a long way in a short period of time.

The current plans for the 61 acres include 3,600 residential units, 420,000 square feet of retail, 2.3 million square feet of office space, and even three casinos with a total of 1,750 rooms. The first mid-rise project of 180 units is expected to range in price from $375,000 to $1 million.

Union Park will be connected to the rest of downtown as an expansion of the Fremont Street Experience by way of the Plaza Casino. This passage will connect the downtown casinos and the Civic Center with all of the project within Union Park.

Recently, the project was accepted as a pilot program for the United States Green Building Council's LEED program (see next page). This neighborhood development program will create an environmentally friendly community.

SoHo Lofts

SoHo Lofts was the first high-rise condominium in downtown Las Vegas. It is also the first building developed by Sam Cherry, who has just recently completed his second project and has a third high-rise towr on the way.

Cherry's entrepreneurial aspirations began early in his life; at the mere age of 15, he used his earnings as a golf caddie to buy a vending machine business, and a year later sold the business for twice the initial investment. He dropped out of high school to begin working with his future father-in-law Harris Ritoff, and invested in Ritoff's real estate projects. When Cherry turned 18, he began buying his own properties, and by 22, he had $1 million in assets.

Soon Cherry turned his attention to the opportunities that downtown Las Vegas offered. He believes that the corridor between Main Street and Las Vegas

What is LEED?

The most recognized organization regulating and certifying green building standards is the U.S. Green Building Council and their Leadership in Energy and Environmental Design (LEED) Green Building Rating System™.

According to the system, a building's design, construction, and operation must work to maximize human and environmental health by setting standards for site development, water savings, energy efficiency, materials selection, and indoor environmental quality to attain certification.

A LEED-certified building can reduce energy consumption from 30 to 70 percent, carbon output by 35 percent, water usage from 30 to 50 percent, and waste from 50 to 90 percent. These are substantial reductions that benefit both the environment and our pocket books.

The United States spends about one-quarter of the national electricity budget on lighting, which translates to more then $37 billion annually. However, technologies developed during the past 10 years can help the U.S. cut lighting costs 40 to 80 percent while enhancing lighting quality and reducing environmental impacts. On a household scale, green residences can save hundreds of dollars annually on energy-efficient lighting alone, not to mention other savings through increased efficiency in appliances and heating and cooling systems.

Moreover, both federal and state governments have started encouraging green building and energy efficiency by offering tax incentives for buyers. Many power companies offer refunds or discounts for households using energy-efficient technology like solar panels and special light bulbs. These tax breaks and lower utility bills indicate that green living is not only good for our environment, but also increasingly affordable.

In the true nature of green thinking, vertical living is an optimal situation for environmental efforts. Mid- and high-rise buildings leave a small footprint on the earth. Unlike track housing and master-planned communities, a fraction of the land is used. By building upwards, a large number of people can live on a small parcel of land, and the land saved can make way for parks, recreation, and environmental preservation areas, all of which look beautiful from a balcony several stories up.

Green vertical residences usually range between 800 and 2,500 square feet in size and can cost anywhere from the mid-$300,000s to over $2 million. They often have significantly lower Homeowner Association fees due to the energy savings in the common areas, and minimal required property maintenance.

Green residences have proven to appreciate in value more quickly than traditionally constructed homes. According to a 1998 Environmental Protection Agency study, for every one dollar a property's annual energy costs were reduced, the property's value increased $10 to $20. So, for example, by saving $1,500 on energy costs every year, the value of the home would rise by $15,000 to $30,000.

As the costs of the green technologies continue to decline and the government encourages energy-efficient building, the quality and number of green vertical residences will continue to grow. As people learn about LEED certification, environmentally friendly residences will become more attractive to buyers than traditionally constructed homes.

Boulevard, and between Charleston Boulevard and Fremont Street, "will just grow to the sky."

The SoHo Lofts' 112 units are sold out. It has a variety of floor plans that range from 1,336 to 1,855 square feet. Prices began at $379,000 and topped out at more than $2.7 million for penthouses. In keeping with an urban design, the first floor of the tower has 4,000 square feet of retail space. Cherry says this space is important for developing a sense of community and the SoHo-type lifestyle.

Hint: *The City of Las Vegas has put a lot of money into improving the street-scape of Fourth Street, which borders SoHo. According to City officials, another street bordering the property, Hoover Street, will receive a face-lift. Look at where the City is planning on spending money; areas with government attention can often turn from bad to good relatively quickly and, as a result, property values in the area could increase. Look for areas of redevelopment for great investment opportunities.*

Newport Lofts

Even before construction was in full swing at SoHo Lofts, more than 1,000 people contacted Sam Cherry and his associates, expressing interest in his next project, Newport Lofts.

Newport Lofts is a 335-foot-tall, 23-story building on the corner of Casino Center Boulevard and Hoover

Avenue. Its design and blue-tinted glass exterior are inspired by Southern California architecture. As of this writing, the construction is complete and the first residents are getting settled.

The project's inspiration and its name may be attributed to the firm with whom Cherry partnered for this project, Seegmiller Partners real estate developer based in Newport, California.

Newport Lofts offers ten floor plans that range from 900 to 1,600 square feet. There are also 12 two-story penthouses, which cost as much as $1.9 million. Meanwhile, the prices for the other units started at $450,000.

On the roof of the building, with a full view of Las Vegas, are a fitness center, pool, garden, and the Skyroom Clubhouse containing a lounge, movie room, and billiard tables.

Hint: *As with SoHo Lofts, many of the buyers of units in Newport Lofts intended to rent them out. This is a good strategy for long-term investment, but it comes with a mortgage payment. Even though the renters will be paying the majority of the price, make sure that you can support the full mortgage if the unit is vacant or a payment is missed or skipped.*

Stanhi

Stanhi will be Sam Cherry's third building. As of this writing construction has not begun on the project, but it has been designed and plans are in the works. While SoHo Lofts has a deco/Manhattan feel and Newport Lofts has a Southern California feel, Stanhi will have a modern Asian design.

The 425 condominium units of this 45-story tower will range in size from 700 to 1,500 square feet. Buyers will have the option of purchasing adjoining units to create larger "super-sized" residences.

Hint: *It is always a good idea to research the developer. Cherry Development has proven itself with the success of SoHo and Newport Lofts. With two sold-out and completed projects and another following suit, Cherry Development has a lot of momentum.*

As construction costs continue to rise, so will unit prices. However, an experienced developer is more likely to adapt to a changing market and offer the appropriate incentives required to sell units. Look for the incentives offered by Cherry Development for their Stanhi project.

Streamline Tower

The entertainment district, located at the east end of Fremont Street, has witnessed the opening of several new nightclubs and other entertainment facilities in the past year. Streamline Tower LLC purchased the Golden Inn and Travel Inn near the Neonopolis for $6.4 million, and demolished the Golden Inn to make room for the 21-floor condominium tower with 275 units and

24,000 square feet of commercial space. Prices began in the $400,000s.

Developer Patrick McCourt has more than 30 years of experience in real estate development, with projects in Oregon, Washington State, and Alaska. The builder, Martin-Harris Construction, is one of the largest construction companies in Nevada.

Hint: *Streamline will be the tallest building and the only condo project in the area. Properties around the entertainment district are becoming more attractive to developers. Streamline has at least a year's head start before any other projects will be completed in the area, and its accessibility to the growing downtown entertainment district will keep units appreciating for years after it is completed.*

Juhl

The development company Citymark Development, known for its distinctive properties in the Gas Lamp District of San Diego, is currently building a $170 million mixed-use project in downtown Las Vegas.

The design of the downtown city blocks lends itself to smaller, loft-style projects. Juhl units will be one- and two-story lofts ranging from 600 to 2,200 square feet. Juhl's towers rise six to 15 stories and consist of 341 lofts with 10-foot ceilings.

Hint: *Developers such as Citymark were an essential part of making a rundown area, the Gas Lamp District, into one of the most highly sought-after places to live in San Diego. Citymark has a good eye for areas with potential, and Juhl promises to offer a fresh urban setting in downtown Las Vegas. As downtown becomes a vibrant community, Juhl will be a key property in the area; thus, units should appreciate well.*

Verge

Standing just off the Spaghetti Bowl at Main Street and Bonanza Road, Verge offers residents easy access to Interstate 15 and Highway 95. Better yet, Verge's units are relatively low-priced for this market; 60 percent of the units were originally priced under $400,000, with over half of those priced less than $200,000.

This $135 million project will consist of eight stories of units over two levels of underground parking. There will also be more than 30,000 square feet of commercial space. A portion of the office space, 40 suites, will be reserved for residents.

Hint: *Verge is pioneering this particular area of downtown, which is notorious for being a "rough neighborhood." This partially explains why the units are being sold for well under what they could be worth if the area is rejuvenated. The developer is hoping that Verge will open doors to other projects that will help improve the area. Keep your eyes open for news on* *plans for the area. If the area shows improvement, look to invest in the early phases, while the prices are low.*

Chapter Four
South Strip

Las Vegas Valley CONDO MAP

South Strip

Existing

40 Loft 5
41 Park Avenue
42 Manhattan
43 Boca Raton

Under Construction

44 ONE Las Vegas

Pre-selling

45 L5
46 Brickwater

Cancelled

47 Urban Village

Map Area:

APPLIED ANALYSIS

Las Vegas Valley CONDO MAP

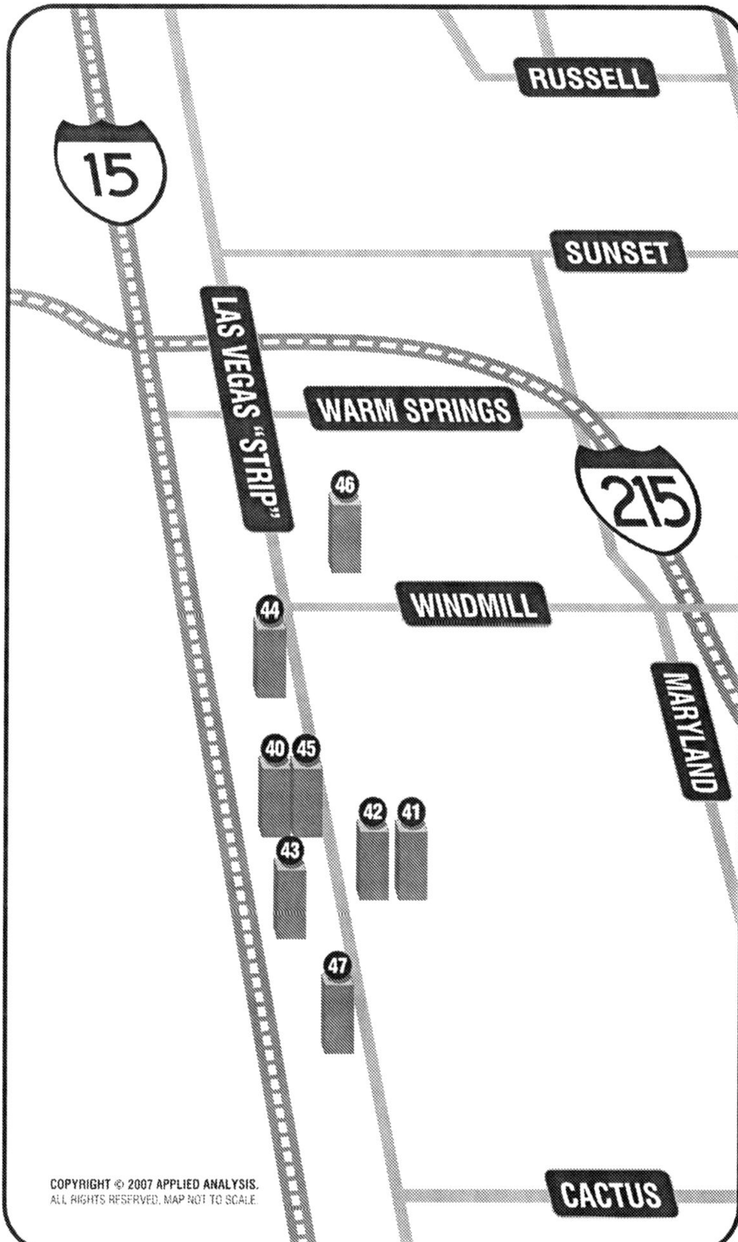

The Resort Corridor Expands

The land along Las Vegas Boulevard south of McCarran Airport is one of the fastest developing sectors in Las Vegas.

In recent years the land south of Mandalay Bay lay void of major projects, but today, it is filling up quickly with casinos and mid-rise and low-rise condominium projects as well as timeshare properties.

This year, not only will new residential projects become available, but there will also be major retail outlets. Town Square will bring a new retail experience to Las Vegas with 1.5 million square feet of shopping.

Labeled the South Strip, land prices along this stretch of Las Vegas Boulevard made the area attractive to developers who wanted to offer affordable products to people wanting to live near the Strip. Now the area has taken on a life of its own and has emerged as a destination unto itself.

Park Avenue

Park Avenue spearheaded the development of the

South Strip. Years before any other major development, Amland Development anticipated the growth along Las Vegas Boulevard south of the airport.

Though technically a low-rise, Park Avenue broke ground as the first affordable project close to the Strip. While prices were first offered in the high $100,000s, they quickly rose with the increased demand. In fact, Park Avenue held the title of the fastest selling community in the United States when it first opened.

Hint: *When there is a successful project in a relatively undeveloped area, it can appreciate quickly and help increase the value of surrounding properties. As the values of the Park Avenue units rose, so did the prices of the units available in surrounding projects like Manhattan. Sometimes it pays off to take the risk of investing in an undeveloped area.*

ONE Las Vegas

With the success of Park Avenue, Amland Development partnered with the B.S.R. Group to develop ONE Las Vegas.

ONE Las Vegas will consist of five towers ranging in height from 18 to 21 stories. There are also plans for a 200-room hotel, a 200-room condo-hotel, and shops to create a whole community on one campus.

Prices for the condominium units originally ranged from the $400,000s for an 850-square-foot unit to $1.8 million for a 2,850-square-foot penthouse. The first two towers are topped off and residents are expected to begin moving in in the spring of 2008.

Hint: *Instead of pursuing investors, ONE Las Vegas seeks buyers who are interested in becoming residents of the community. These potential buyers include those who want to shorten their commute to work or to the entertainment offered by the Strip. Residents will have easy access to shopping and nearby casinos and resorts.*

Manhattan

The Manhattan condominiums are built around a "Central Park," which was originally planned to be much larger than it is. To cover the cost of the rising construction prices, it was necessary to sell a section of the project's land, resulting in a reduction in the size of the common areas.

Without the views of other projects like Turnberry Place or Panorama, Manhattan was designed to be an oasis where, instead of looking outward, the community looks inward, toward the landscaped common area. Alexander Edelstein of Gemstone Development likens the concept to Harvard Yard, where students leave their dormitories at Harvard University and step directly onto grass.

Edelstein says, "We look at land like a sculptor looking at a rock. We see what the rock can produce and envision what the South Strip will look like in the years to come. We were able to follow such a tight schedule because we have assembled people who excel in their fields of expertise."

Edelstein feels luxury condos like Turnberry Place are sensitive to market changes and cater to people living outside Las Vegas. He also thinks that a more moderately priced project like Manhattan will sustain the interest of casino employees and others who wish to avoid long commutes or want to be closer to the core of Las Vegas.

"Look at Miami," said Edelstein. "Everyone wants to live near the ocean. So you have all these high-rises lined up along the beach. In Vegas, the Strip is our ocean. People want to live near it. The closer you are to the Strip, the more you expect to pay for the luxury."

Hint: *The fact that most of the available units sold during the pre-sale period speaks to the demand for their product. In fact, all of the units were sold in 28 days, making Manhattan Las Vegas also one of the fastest-selling communities in the country. The sales office is currently reselling units for initial buyers. They expected 25 percent of the original buyers to "flip" the units and resell them without moving in.*

Boca Raton

Boca Raton Condominiums are being built in the same neighborhood as the Manhattan condominiums just south of the Las Vegas Strip.

On opening weekend, Boca Raton enjoyed similar results as Manhattan, bringing in $40 million in sales for the 173 units that were available.

When the $400 million construction project is completed it will consist of four seven-story buildings with 756 units ranging in price from $200,000 to more than $1 million. Each building will have two stories of underground parking.

Boca Raton offers buyers a ground floor opportunity in the quickly developing South Strip area. New casinos are opening and construction is beginning on nearby shopping complexes. Because of its location and amenities, Boca Raton attracts both local full-time residents and part-time residents looking for a second home in Las Vegas.

Hint: *Boca Raton invested a substantial amount into its marketing campaign. Do not let the marketing interfere with your assessment of the units. Just because you see ten billboards for the same project does not mean it is successful—just that it has managed to secure marketing funds. However, the execution of an effective marketing campaign, like Boca Raton's, does show strength in the developer, which will be reflected in other facets of the project. Boca Raton's architecture sets it apart from other projects. Even as the first residents were moving in, the project became a popular spot among photographers for photo shoots.*

Loft 5

Merging design elements from New York, Los Angeles, and San Diego, the low-rise condominium project known as Loft 5 has multi-level lofts with 20-foot ceilings and penthouses with private sky decks.

The design and architecture of the project is modern minimalist. Rick Firmine, a partner of the development team m_space development, defines "Loftstyle™" as the union of "cutting-edge sophistication with modern loft living."

The developers of Loft 5 are conscious of the impact such projects have on the environment. For this reason, they provide more open community space (nearly two acres) than is required or even typical in condominium projects. Other environmentally friendly features include bamboo-wood flooring and Balsatina natural stone countertops. With two pools and two "lifestyle centers," residents enjoy amenities that promote healthy lifestyles.

Prices initially ranged from $550,000 to $720,000, with floor plans from 1,234 to 1,848 square feet. Loft 5 has been a successful property, selling out in six months, and residents have begun moving in.

Hint: *Located along the growing South Strip, Loft 5 promises to be a hub for the younger professional crowd working on or near the Strip. The modern building design and amenities make this project attractive to those wanting to live close to the action.*

L5

Following the success of Loft 5, the same developers are building L5 on Pebble Road at Las Vegas Boulevard.

The new development will feature live/work flats and garden flats on the first floor. The garden flats open directly into secluded garden areas, which open into common courtyards, simultaneously offering privacy and community access. Other units feature double-height lofts and three-tiered penthouses.

The 284 units will be spread over three six-story buildings that are connected to create five garden courtyards. The residences will range in size from 600 to over 2,000 square feet, and prices range from $180,000 to $800,000.

The design influences of L5 are similar to those of Loft 5. L5 not only reflects a minimalist design, but is inspired by interlocking opposites. The Graham Downes Architecture firm hopes that the property will evolve with the personality of the residents. For this reason, they offer over 40 different floor plans and encourage owners to define their own living spaces.

Hint: *L5 is a scaled-back, more affordable version of Loft 5. It also has the same developer and is based on similar concepts. These elements make L5 an attractive buy for those who cannot afford the neighboring Loft 5. With a similar look and location, Loft 5 will protect L5's price and appreciation.*

Brickwater

The Brickwater is being built near the 215 Beltway and Interstate 15 interchange. The price point for these condominiums will be relatively affordable at $330 per square foot. There are 11 different floor plans with units ranging from 849 to 1,550 square feet. The 256 units will be sold in two phases, each offering 178 units.

The courtyard will feature a swimming pool that is fed by a stream flowing from a fountain wall at the complex's entry. The exterior will be principally red brick, as the name suggests, giving it a sturdy and comfortable look. The structure is primarily marketed to working couples who will be full-time residents. The project is expected to be open for occupancy in 2008.

Hint: *While this project is currently relatively unknown, expect word to spread as it nears completion. Brickwater's wood-frame construction yields reasonable pricing, which means this project will be attainable for a larger segment of the population.*

Chapter Five
Suburban Projects

The Emergence of Mid-Rise and Low-Rise

The same forces driving vertical construction along the Strip and downtown apply to mid-rise and low-rise condominiums in the suburbs. As land and construction prices rise, the notion of vertical communities becomes more attractive. This is especially true for parcels of land that are relatively small but offer great views or proximity to attractions.

Many of the suburban vertical projects create mini-downtowns that offer retail, dining, office space, and entertainment within walking distance of the residences. This new town-center concept is emerging in many places throughout the United States as malls and strip-malls are replaced by regional live, work, shop, and play centers. While they may lack the charm of traditional downtowns that have been revitalized, the new town-centers offer a sense of community.

Usually, a new town-center provides high-density housing such as mid-rise or low-rise condominiums with "streets" where residents can easily walk to shopping, dining, or a meeting over a cup of coffee. In Las Vegas, these communities offer an alternative to suburban sprawl and long commutes. They also offer an alternative to those who cannot afford similar products on the Strip.

Traditionally, investors have been reluctant to purchase vertical residencies in the suburbs. First, they recognize that people who live in the suburbs seek the suburban lifestyle, which includes a single-family home with a yard.

Second, if an investor wants to "flip" the unit, the pool of potential buyers is larger for a Strip or downtown property because most people living in new town-centers choose their location based on the distance to work, not solely on the attractiveness of the product itself. In other words, if a person lives in Centennial Hills, he or she is more likely to choose a nearby mixed-use community than one in Summerlin or Henderson.

Third, frequently the residences in the new town-centers are still expensive. Because the product is relatively new, it is unclear what type of returns an investor could make on the investment.

Finally, we must recognize that some investors choose investments for less than rational reasons. A Strip property is much "sexier" than a smaller project in the suburbs; telling your friends that you own a condominium at the Palms is much more exciting than telling them you own one along the 215 curve.

Of course, investors shouldn't let emotions dictate purchases. Careful consideration of the new town-centers will present many investment opportunities, as well as attractive live/work spaces.

The following projects are divided between projects east of the Strip and those that are located west of the Strip and I-15.

Las Vegas Valley CONDO MAP

Green Valley & Henderson

Existing

48 The District at Green Valley

Under Construction

49 Vantage Lofts
50 Stephanie Village

Pre-selling

51 Green Valley Lofts

Planned/Proposed

52 Trophy Towers

Map Area:

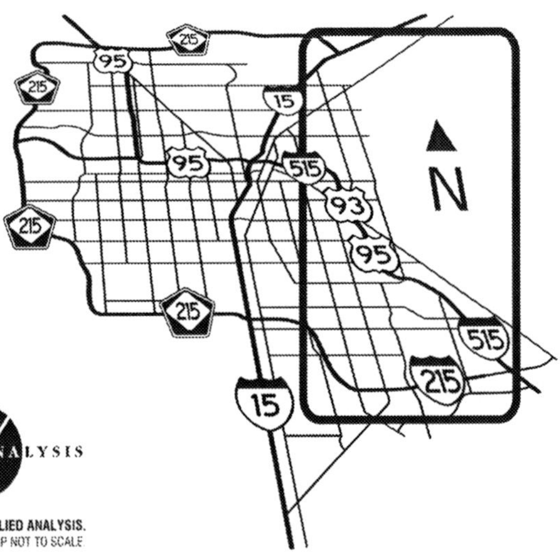

APPLIED ANALYSIS

Las Vegas Valley CONDO MAP

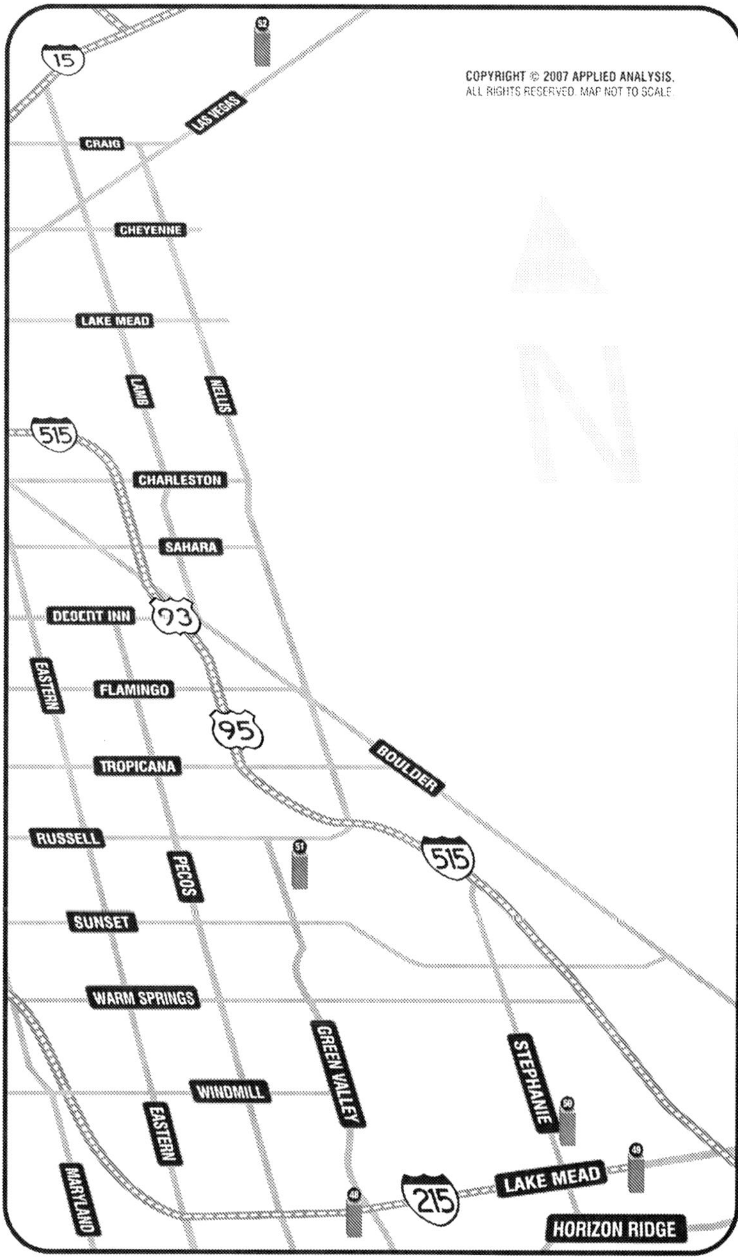

Green Valley & Henderson

The District at Green Valley Ranch

The District at Green Valley Ranch is a good example of a new town-center; it consists of shops surrounding the Green Valley Ranch Resort and Casino, resembling a scaled-down traditional main street with shops lining the "street" and people living above the shops. Of course, in this case, the shops are higher-end than the traditional dime store, and the restaurants are more upscale than the hometown café. Similarly, the living quarters above the shops are more luxurious than most traditional town-centers.

The 88 units range in size from 875 to 1,800 square feet. Many units have rooftop gardens and other amenities. Residents can use the pool at the Green Valley Ranch Resort and Casino.

The second phase of the District is now open, with a Whole Foods Market, Cheesecake Factory, and other retail and office spaces. Theoretically, a resident of the District would rarely drive because offices, shopping, and entertainment are within walking distance.

Hint: *This is the first significant mixed-use development in the suburbs. There are limited resale opportunities because buyers enjoy its location next to Green Valley Ranch, shops, and excellent dining.*

Stephanie Village

Stephanie Village is another good example of one of the new town-centers in development. Located in Henderson near several malls and casinos, Stephanie Village is designed to be a town unto itself.

Stephanie Village will include ten buildings with offices and retail spaces distributed throughout. However, only about a third of the space is dedicated to residences. The ground floors are dedicated to retail and commercial establishments, with the residences located in the three levels above businesses.

One two-story building will contain a clubhouse for the residents. It will feature a gym, a business center, and even a movie theater. There will also be an outdoor amphitheater and two outdoor common areas for recreation and socializing.

There have been three significant demographics interested in investing in Stephanie Village residences. First, young singles have expressed an interest in the carefree living Stephanie Village offers. Second, young professional couples without children are attracted to the amenities of a mixed-use property. Finally, "empty-nesters" seek comfortable properties for downsizing their homes.

The 466 residential units begin at less than $300,000 and top out at $7,225,000 for 2,295-square-foot units. The developers say their new urbanist design is responsible for these relatively reasonable prices. Stephanie Village is currently under construction and is scheduled to begin opening in mid-2008.

Hint: *People seeking a live/work residence and those who want to be located close to work will be attracted to this project. The mixed-use nature of this property will help retain the value of the units.*

Vantage Lofts

Vantage Lofts, which will offer a "minimalist, modern" design, is another example of bringing urban living to Henderson.

Located in the Black Hills in Henderson, Vantage Lofts' prices started in the $400,000s for units ranging from 1,000 to 2,800 square feet. The 20-foot floor-to-ceiling glass windows will display panoramic views of the Las Vegas Valley.

The first phase, which includes three five-story buildings, was expected to be completed by the end of 2007. The buildings will have parking garages in the basement and first level, single-story flats on the second level, and two-story lofts on the third and fourth levels. There will also be brownstone-style homes on the property.

Hint: *This project should be considered by those wanting to move in immediately, and those wanting a quick return on their investment. Its location is attractive to buyers because it has quick access to the 215 and 95 highways. It is also near Lake Las Vegas Resort. Better yet, the developer is an established development company with its own general contractor. This record will ensure quality construction. It should also alleviate some investors' concerns about how well the property will maintain its value and how well it will appreciate in the long term.*

Green Valley Lofts

Green Valley Lofts will be located on Green Valley Parkway with panoramic views of the Las Vegas Strip and mountains. The five-story building will include 44 residential open-space condominiums with compatible retail and office units on the first floor.

There will be a rooftop, glass-enclosed spa, and fitness facility attached to an open-deck pool and Jacuzzi, private subterranean parking, and some of the most advanced building technologies available today.

The building will substantially reduce energy costs for tenants and minimize the impact of construction and maintenance on the environment. Green Valley Lofts will qualify for the coveted Energy-Star Rating and will receive LEED (Leadership in Energy and Environmental Design) certification, as a mixed-use residential building in Las Vegas.

The "whole-building" design creates integrated systems that act as an "envelope" and take advantage of solar technology and energy efficiencies, including photovoltaic cells on the roof of the building to convert sunlight into energy.

The 44 units will have bamboo floors, recycled glass counter tops, and non-toxic paint. The windows will use NASA technology that protects astronauts from heat and radiation, blocking 99 percent of UV rays. Other technologies include tank-less hot water heaters and efficient lighting.

Green Valley Lofts' pricing will range from the low $300,000s to the mid $600,000s for the one- and two-bedroom units. The penthouse suites will start in the low $800,000s. There are also federal and state tax incentives for owning an energy-efficient home.

Hint: *This project offers an attractive combination of suburban living in the heart of Green Valley. Residents enjoy property amenities as well as easy access to shopping, restaurants, gyms, and the Green Valley Ranch Resort. With the LEED certification as well as the beautiful Strip views, there is a strong appreciation potential with this property.*

Trophy Towers

Perhaps appealing to a different clientele than other vertical projects, Trophy Towers will stand next to the Las Vegas Motor Speedway in the far northeast of

Las Vegas Valley. When originally submitted, the plan called for 127 unit towers that overlook the first turn of the 1.5-mile oval track. The units will range from 1,750 to 3,500 square feet and will have views of the track and the Strip. Prices are expected to range from $500,000 to $4 million.

Speedway Motorsports Inc. is expected to move one of its annual Cup races to the Las Vegas Speedway as early as 2008, which will increase the demand for this property. Developer Bruton Smith notes that the condominium units will not be primary homes for the buyers. They are intended more for entertainment purposes, as a glorified tailgate party. Owners can invite friends to their condominium to watch the race and celebrate.

Hint: *This project has encountered resistance by the nearby Nellis Air Force Base, thus delaying the project. However, it will be a great buy for those interested in auto racing. Residences will be a key attraction during NASCAR events. The property will function more like a condo-hotel since few people will live there on a permanent basis.*

Las Vegas Valley CONDO MAP

Summerlin & Southwest

Existing

53 C2 Lofts
54 One Queensridge Place

Under Construction

55 The Mercer
56 Manhattan West
57 Sullivan Square
58 The Village at Queensridge

Pre-selling

59 Pinnacle
60 Mira Villa
61 SpaLofts
62 Echelon at Centennial Hills
63 Promenada at Rainbow

Planned/Proposed

64 C2 Lofts Upper West Side

Cancelled

65 Red Rock Resort Residences
66 The Curve
67 Spanish View Towers

Map Area:

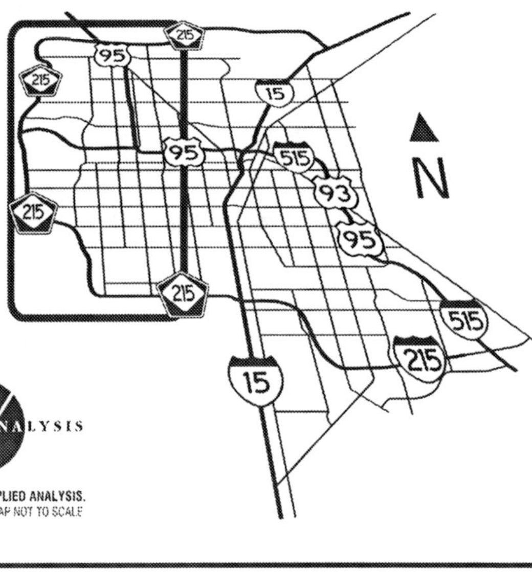

APPLIED ANALYSIS

Las Vegas Valley CONDO MAP

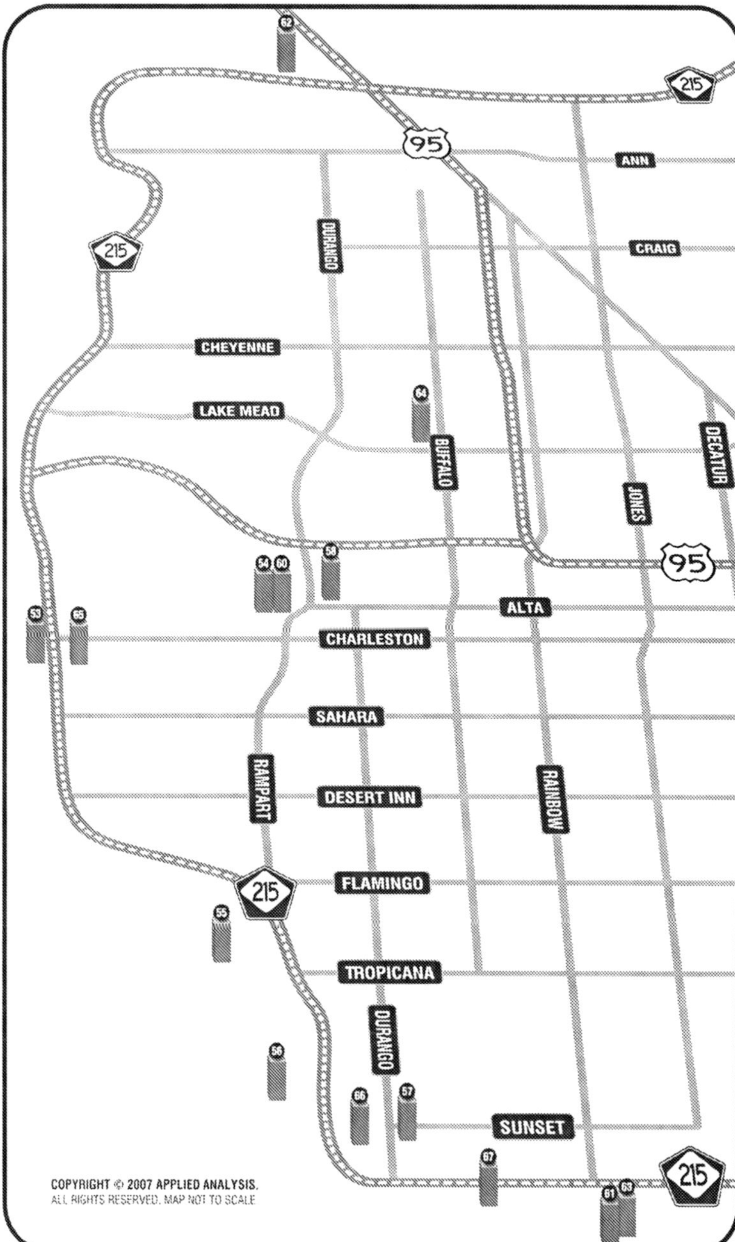

Summerlin & Southwest

C2 Lofts

Directly across the 215 freeway from Red Rock Resort in Summerlin stands C2 Lofts. This project has two five-story buildings with residences above the first-level parking garage and retail space. The 100 units are priced from the $700,000s to more than $1.2 million for 1,400 to 2,602 square feet of living space.

Besides the usual amenities one would expect from such a project, the buildings have "roof gardens" from which residents can enjoy the stunning city views while socializing with their neighbors. These common spaces have lounging areas, barbecues, fireplaces, and restrooms. Additionally, the purchase price of a unit includes an executive-level membership to Red Rock Country Club.

Due to the positive response to the first project, the developer, Christopher Company, is planning a second C2 Lofts community near U.S. 95 and West Lake Mead Boulevard. This community, C2 Lofts Upper West Side, will be much larger, with 900 units.

Hint: *C2 Lofts is a beautiful property. The units have high ceilings and many impressive amenities, offering an urban loft style in a residential neighborhood. Perhaps the most important aspect of C2 Lofts is its location close to the Red Rock Casino and the coming Summerlin Center.*

One Queensridge Place

One Queensridge Place rises above the eastern side of Summerlin. Resting against the canyon walls of Badlands Golf Course, One Queensridge Place offers spectacular views unmatched anywhere else in the Las Vegas Valley.

This view and the amenities come at a price. When sales began for the first two towers, the cheapest unit among the 219 residences was $1.6 million for a 2,000-square-foot unit, with penthouses starting at $4 million. Residents recently began moving into these 18-story towers.

In 2004, the City of Las Vegas approved 385 residences in four towers for this site. The third tower will be 18 stories, and the fourth will be 14 stories.

One Queensridge Place is located near the Boca Park shops and across the street from the Suncoast Hotel and Casino. The coming Village at Queensridge shopping center will offer added convenience to the residents of One Queensridge Place.

Hint: *Many Summerlin residents are trading in their luxury homes for a lower-maintenance lifestyle. These people want to remain near the amenities of Summerlin while adopting a lock-and-leave lifestyle; for them, One Queensridge is an ideal solution, allowing them to maintain a luxurious lifestyle without the hassles.*

The Village at Queensridge

Located caddy-corner to One Queensridge, The Village at Queensridge will be a boutique shopping center with two five-story condominium towers and one ten-story tower. The 340 units will range in price from $600,000 to over $1 million.

Hint: *Pre-construction pricing is still available for this project. Units are priced lower than One Queensridge across the street, but provide many of the same amenities. The Village at Queensridge will be conveniently located among a new high-end shopping center that will be sure to attract residents, similarly to how the District has become a successful property.*

Mira Villa

Located just north of One Queensridge Place, Mira Villa will offer a similar location at a more reasonable price (beginning at $750,000 and topping out more than $1.2 million). Westmark Homes is building 8 five-story buildings with units ranging in size from 2,071 to

3,917 square feet. Balconies of some units are as large as 1,372 square feet.

Mira Villa is located across the road from the JW Marriot Resort and Rampart Casino, near the TPC Canyons Golf Course. It stands along the cliffs above the Angel Park Golf Course. Because of its height and the golf course, many units have an unobstructed view of the Las Vegas Valley, while others look over the golf courses and up at the Red Rock Mountains.

Hint: *Mira Villa is only one stoplight away from One Queensridge. Similar to the larger, more expensive project, Mira Villa is also on a golf course and next to a casino. These residences are reasonably priced and therefore attractive to a larger market. For commuters, this property is easily accessible from the Summerlin Parkway.*

The Mercer

The Mercer is a mixed-use project that includes three story and four-story buildings. It is being built at the intersection of Tropicana Avenue and Grand Canyon Drive.

The $50 million project will include 113 units with sizes ranging from 800 to 2,370 square feet of living space. These residences feature dedicated work areas complete with bookshelves and computer spaces. This means the second and third bedrooms will not have to be used as home offices.

At roughly $300 per square foot, prices range from $229,000 to $699,000, making the Mercer one of the more affordable projects in Las Vegas. These price levels do not reflect a lack of amenities and design features; the units will have wood floors, stainless-steel appliances, and access to semi-private elevators. The project is expected to be completed by mid-2008.

Hint: *The Mercer is an attractive project in the growing southwest area. The developers are paying close attention to details, finishes, and floor plans. While farther from Highway 215 than some other projects in the area, the Mercer offers elements not found in other properties.*

Manhattan West

Developer Alex Edelstein is improving upon the original design and amenities of the Manhattan community on the South Strip. With Manhattan West, he expanded his mission of saving residents' time and improving their physical and social health.

Manhattan West is located on Russell Road, west of 215. When completed, there will be 700 units spread throughout the 12 buildings. The buildings themselves will range in height from four to nine stories surrounding a courtyard, similar to the layout of the original Manhattan community. The cost per square foot for the units is over $300, so the average price for a unit is in the $400,000 range.

To enhance the social atmosphere for the residents, Manhattan West will feature a coffee shop/wine shop in the community. The common areas will also be structured to encourage residents to meet and converse with each other. For instance, all of the barbecues will be located in a centralized space, rather than spread throughout the property, in order to bring neighbors together when they grill their dinners.

Edelstein experimented with this concept in the original Manhattan project and fondly recalls a resident who told him, "I met more people in one week living at Manhattan than I have in 20 years living in Las Vegas."

Hint: *The original Manhattan project has been successful, and its reputation will easily transfer to Manhattan West. Manhattan West offers an excellent location and improved amenities. People will embrace the lifestyle that Manhattan West delivers, and there are plenty of buying opportunities with this property.*

Echelon at Centennial Hills

Not to be confused with Echelon Place being built on the Strip, Echelon at Centennial Hills is a low-rise community in the northwest part of Las Vegas. It is located just off North Durango Drive near the intersection of Interstates 215 and 95.

The $200 million project will include six four-story buildings with units ranging from $400,000 to more than $1.5 million. The 11 different floor plans include units sized from 1,064 to 4,164 square feet.

Hint: *This project is located some distance from the core of the city. This means it appeals to a different market than downtown projects or new town-center projects; it offers those in the northwest suburbs an urban experience far from the lights and glitz of the Strip.*

Promenada at Rainbow

Cabi Developers purchased 15 acres of land for $15 million at the intersection of Warm Springs Road and Rainbow Boulevard. Here they will build a mixed-use, mid-rise development called Promenada at Rainbow.

The community will consist of 479 residences and over 60,000 square feet of retail shopping. Residents and guests will be able to park their cars in the underground parking garage—a rarity in Las Vegas. The units are priced at $380 per square foot; so an 828-square-foot unit would fall in the mid-$300,000 range.

Hint: *This is another good example of a suburban condominium project. The Florida developers bring the architectural and design elements of Florida to Southwest Las Vegas.*

Sullivan Square

Sullivan Square brings the feel of vintage downtown Chicago to the Las Vegas suburbs. The exterior of the buildings resembles the old, familiar buildings of another area, and the streets and park are also reminiscent of a time when community could be found in urban centers.

When it is finished, Sullivan Square will have over 1,300 residences spanning six different types of living options: high-rise towers, condominiums, lofts, townhomes, brownstones, and live/work spaces.

The stores lining the streets will house 25 shops and services, including restaurants, pubs, cafés, a fresh fish market, butcher shop, and bakery, all huddled around a one-and-a-half-acre park.

Hint: *While other vertical projects failed around the 215 Curve, this project will succeed because it will create an entire neighborhood rather than just residential towers. It also has solid financial backing and lenders who supported the experienced developer, GSG Development. Sullivan Square will transform how mixed-use projects are developed in Las Vegas. There are some pre-construction opportunities with this project.*

Chapter Six
Condo-Hotels and Fractionals

Second-Home Alternatives

Condo-Hotels

Condo-hotels, a hybrid of hotels and condominiums, are a relatively new product in Las Vegas. These developments became common in South America over a decade ago, and can now be found in several U.S. destinations, including ski resorts in Colorado and Utah as well as beach communities in South Florida (home to 30 condo-hotels under construction or recently completed). Worldwide, condo-hotels have an even longer history, especially in Latin America and Europe.

The basic concept behind a condo-hotel is this: you own the condominium and can use it whenever you want. You also have the option to put your unit into the managed rental pool, at which point the associated management company rents out your unit nightly, similar to a hotel room.

Condo-hotels look and feel like luxury hotel. The units are not only furnished, but they are often designed like high-end hotel suites. The management company typically offers concierge and bellmen services as well as daily housekeeping. There are also pools, spas, restaurants, and bars in the "common areas" of the building.

Condo-hotels appeal to those seeking a second home, and who have an additional interest in generating cash-flow on their property while they are not using it. When the unit is placed into the rental pool, the management company rents the unit to short-term guests and shares a portion of the profits with the owner.

However, the resale market for condo-hotels in Las Vegas is relatively new. Therefore, this product does not have a long-term investment record. Time will be needed to judge the effectiveness of condo-hotels' return on investment.

As investments, condo-hotels have a tricky designation. The 1986 Tax Reform Act repealed many of the tax advantages that traditionally accompany real estate investments. The Securities and Exchange Commission (SEC) considers the condominium property a "security" if the property is sold to the buyer with the expectation of earning money for the buyer or the expectation of receiving tax benefits from the purchase. If this occurs, a securities broker must sell the property. This also makes it easier for the buyer to sue the developer using anti-fraud rules.

To avoid being vulnerable to lawsuits, most developers prohibit their salespeople from discussing the economic and tax benefits of their condo-hotels and rental programs. Salespeople are also prohibited from making projections about how much income a condominium unit will make through the rental program.

The rental programs must be presented as one of many available options. Although it is unlikely that a buyer would choose a different program, they must still have the option to do so. The rental program must be voluntary, as well as separate and distinct from the sales department. Furthermore, the buyer should not be asked to sign an agreement that places the property into the rental program before the binding purchase agreement has been signed. If the developers are asking for this document to be signed prior, they should have written to the SEC and requested that the agency take no action against the project. In response, the SEC would issue a "take no action" letter.

Most people who purchase condo-hotels do so in order to enjoy the benefits of a vacation home while generating revenue on the property when they are not using it. Instead of anticipating a return on your investment, it is better to view this revenue as defraying the expenses of your vacation-home ownership.

Usually, the managing company will keep 50 percent of the proceeds when they rent the owner's unit. Owners will also pay management fees and monthly cleaning fees. Since there are frequently room shortages in Las Vegas, and since conventioneers create a demand for rooms during the week, owners can have some assurance that it will have some occupancy.

Owners also face restrictions on how they can decorate their units. Generally, the participating hotel or management company is responsible for furnishing and decorating the condo-hotel. Owners typically pay periodic assessments to cover new furniture and updates throughout the property.

When it comes to the Unit Rental Program Agreement, there are several aspects to which a potential buyer needs to pay close attention before becoming involved in the rental program:

1. Limitations placed on how often and when you can use the property: Sometimes the management company has black-out periods; this is especially likely in Las Vegas, where major conventions can buy up all available rooms.

2. Split of the rental revenue: Usually, the split is 50/50, but there is some variety in the market.

3. Management fees: These can surprise owners. The fees can range from replacing broken televisions to paying for security visits to the unit.

4. Promotional uses of the unit: Check to see if the management company reserves the right to use your unit for promotional purposes. In these cases, you will not receive your expected income from the property.

5. Number of available units the management company needs available at any one time: Usually the management company requires a certain minimum number of units to be available. When there is such a requirement, there will be rules for ensuring availability.

6. Cleaning schedule: While daily cleaning is likely, there are also scheduled "deep cleanings" that affect the availability of your property to yourself and the rental program.

7. Accounting system: Revenues and costs need to be kept separate for your individual unit. Make sure you understand the accounting system and how profits are counted and distributed.

While investment should not be your main motivation for purchasing a condo-hotel, it is likely that your property will appreciate, especially if you purchase the property during pre-sale phases.

There are many things to consider when purchasing a condo-hotel, and while it may seem like a daunting investment, the risks of owning a condo-hotel and the financial outlays are similar to owning a standard condominium, especially in an expensive location, such as along the Strip.

The Signature at MGM Grand

Following the success of Turnberry Place, Turnberry Associates joined with MGM Grand to build a condo-hotel project on the land that was once an entertainment park. This project, formerly called The Residences at MGM Grand, consists of three 40-story towers with 576 units per tower.

When an owner chooses to place his or her unit in the rental pool, MGM Grand will assign guests to the unit. The units themselves are managed and maintained by MGM Grand, but the towers will have their own, separate amenities, including a fitness center, swimming pool, and concierge services. The MGM Grand, connected via a covered air-conditioned corridor equipped with moving walkways, houses a variety of restaurants, lounges, and entertainment venues.

The units are furnished with everything from linens to tableware. There are custom interior amenities available, such as Sub-Zero refrigerators, Meile appliances, and LCD flat-screen HDTVs. Initially prices ranged from $550,000 for 600-square-foot studios to $2.5 million for 1,500-square-foot two-bedroom units.

Construction has been ahead of schedule because demand has been high for the units. This high demand, coupled with Turnberry Associates' reputation and the convenient proximity to MGM Grand and the Strip, make this a particularly attractive product for people wanting a second or third home in Las Vegas.

Hint: *This is the first major condo-hotel project completed in Las Vegas. Units can now be purchased through individual agents who have a listing of resale properties. There is also a resale office on the premises. Many of the units available for resale come from investors who want to flip their units; these investors are competing with themselves and therefore selling at lower prices than the developer is offering for new units in Tower Three. As a condo-hotel, this project is attractive because it is on the Strip and is* *supported by the MGM-Mirage reservation and marketing machine.*

Platinum

Recognizing the attraction of the "Flamingo Corridor," Platinum offers a "club-like, residential atmosphere" to its owners and their renters. Flamingo Road is quickly becoming a restaurant corridor behind the Strip. Even though it is on Flamingo Road, Platinum faces Koval Lane, making it easier to approach the building.

This condo-hotel offers amenities that include a luxury spa, indoor and outdoor swimming pools, a poolside lounge, a café, a bar, and a restaurant in the lobby. The complex also has a rooftop terrace that offers stunning views of the Strip and the surrounding Las Vegas Valley.

The units themselves range in size from 911 to 2,166 square feet; prices range from the $300,000s to $1 million. Each unit is equipped with a plasma-screen TV, a whirlpool bath, and a private terrace, and owners are allowed to customize their interior furnishings.

The rental program is run by Marcus Resorts & Hotels, a successful luxury-hotel management company located in Milwaukee, Wisconsin.

Hint: *There are many resale opportunities at Platinum. It has a dedicated hotel management company working on marketing and increasing occupancy* *rates. This smaller property offers residency options not available on the Strip. It is also an entirely non-smoking and non-gaming facility.*

Trump International

With all the development excitement occurring in Las Vegas, it was only a matter of time before Donald Trump got serious about putting his mark on the city.

In July 2004, Trump announced that he was building a 64-story tower that would house hotel rooms and apartments. Named the Trump International Hotel and Tower, it is the result of a 50/50 partnership with former New Frontier owner Phil Ruffin. The building is located behind the Fashion Show Mall just off of Las Vegas Boulevard.

The Trump International has more than 1,000 hotel-style units, ranging from 636 to 1,057 square feet. The building also holds 50 penthouses ranging in size from 3,000 to 10,000 square feet. These units will be sold, but owners can lease the space to Trump's management company on a nightly basis. The building should be completed in early 2008.

With the failure of his former wife Ivana's high-rise project, the Trump International will be the second-tallest building in Las Vegas after the Stratosphere. The sky is the limit, so Trump International may not hold this title for long; however, for at least the next few years Donald Trump can be satisfied with the status of his gold glass tower dominating the Las Vegas skyline.

Because of the early success of his project, Trump has plans for a second tower. He expects prices to rise 30 to 35 percent for the next tower.

Hint: *Trump is an international name and brand, making this property attractive to potential buyers from around the world. As a condo-hotel, the name will also pull people interested in staying at the property during their Las Vegas visits. Its location is also attractive—across from the Fashion Show Mall and near the Wynn Resort.*

However, many buyers are not aware that ELAD has purchased the New Frontier and plans to build the Las Vegas version of the Plaza Hotel. In New York City, the condominiums at the Plaza have the highest price per square foot; it is likely that their property in Las Vegas will have a similar distinction. This will have a positive impact on the resale values and future appreciation of units at this project.

A word of caution: people tend to overlook the fact that Trump Towers stands on Frank Sinatra Drive (formerly Industrial Road), which means that the backyard of the Trump Towers is populated with adult entertainment businesses for now.

Palms Place

Once known as a small casino, the Palms' first hotel tower quickly became a major property in Las Vegas. The second tower, known as Fantasy Tower, followed suit. The third tower, Palms Place, is a $600 million 50-story condominium tower that houses 599 units and is connected with the rest of the casino by a 300-foot elevated moving walkway.

Units range from studios of 600 square feet to penthouses of 7,000 square feet. Prices originally began at $500,000 and topped out at $7 million. Units are fully furnished to reflect the tastes and styles of the young, hip crowd that the Palms attracts.

Celebrities, sports stars, actors, major recording artists and high rollers were the first invited to purchase residences at Palms Place. However, as construction costs soared, Palms Place raised its prices six times and counting. The project broke ground in May 2006 immediately following the opening of the second tower, Fantasy Tower.

Hint: *As of this writing, Palms Place is nearing completion. This property has attracted a lot of celebrity attention, especially with its proximity to the world-famous Playboy Club. The celebrity buyers generally do not plan to rent out their units, which means there will be a shortage of units in the reservation program and better occupancy rates for those who plan to rent out their units.*

CityCenter

MGM Mirage is building a $7.8 billion "city center" in the heart of the Strip. The 76-acre master-planned project is the size of the Rockefeller Center, the SoHo neighborhood, and Times Square combined. It will be the largest non-government construction project ever built.

In fact, CityCenter will be so large that it will produce its own electricity. There are plans to build combustion turbines on the property that will generate 9.6 megawatts of electricity.

CityCenter will include two luxury hotels and 550,000 square feet of retail, dining, and entertainment. It will also include two condominium towers with a total of 810 units.

CityCenter will open in stages beginning in 2009 with a goal of completing the whole project by 2010. This will create 12,000 full-time jobs, which will significantly contribute to the Las Vegas economy and increase tourism.

Tony Dennis, the executive vice president of the residential arm of CityCenter, says that while demand for condominium units has slowed down, demand still outpaces supply.

Vdara is the first tower to take reservations. At press time, units were expected to begin at $500,000 for studio residences, each with approximately 500 square feet of living space. The tower will also include one- and two-bedroom penthouses as large as 1,850 square feet. There will be 1,543 units in this 50-story tower.

The two Veer towers will stand 35 stories high, each with 335 residences ranging in size from 500 to 3,200 square feet. The top of the Veer towers will feature an infinity-edge pool with cabanas and a spa, where residents will be able to entertain guests.

The hotel Mandarin Oriental will feature 227 condominium units on its upper floors, ranging in size from 1,000 to 4,100 square feet. Residents will be able to enjoy the luxury and sophistication that Mandarin Oriental hotels offer while remaining separate from the public spaces—the owners of condominiums will have their own entrance and a separate valet parking service.

As plans for CityCenter take shape, look for more exciting features to attract residents and investors.

Hint: *This project will set the bar for other condominium and condo-hotel developments in Las Vegas. Because of its size, it will continue to attract buyer interest for years to come. These residences are at the heart of the Strip and all its attractions.*

Cosmopolitan

Standing between CityCenter and the Bellagio, the Cosmopolitan will be a condo-hotel managed by Hyatt, under its Grand Hyatt brand, giving the hotel company the Strip location it has long desired.

The Cosmopolitan will offer 3,000 rooms, 2,000 of which will be offered for sale as condo-hotel units. The two residential towers will stand 600 feet taller than the Eiffel Tower at Paris Las Vegas across the street from the project.

Below the towers will be a 70,000-square-foot casino and 4 million square feet of pedestrian-friendly shopping, dining, and entertainment including the Cosmo Beach Club, a five-acre pool deck that offers dining, and a night club overlooking the Strip.

The Cosmopolitan is unique in that, unlike CityCenter, it is privately owned and financed. There will be no public stock offerings or bond financing to raise money for its construction.

The Cosmopolitan will be built on a small site, though it will have more rooms per acre than any other resort property on the Strip. This distinction was accomplished by going ten floors underground for parking—a notion unheard of in Las Vegas until now. The clever use of space means that the Cosmopolitan will have more money invested into each square foot than any other project on the Strip.

As of this writing, most of the units have been reserved at prices ranging from $600,000 to as much as $5 million. Fewer than 10 percent of these buyers are from Las Vegas; most are from California, though people from around the world have also shown an interest in the project.

Grand Hyatt will operate the condo-hotel program as well as the 1,000 standard hotel rooms also located at the Cosmopolitan. Not only will the Cosmopolitan give Hyatt a much-coveted space on the Strip, but it will also give the individual owners the advantages of world-class reservation and hospitality services.

Hint: *This building is a great example of Manhattanizing Las Vegas. Because of its small lot size, the developers had to maximize the building design to deliver the best use of the property. The location of this project will make it attractive to many buyers.*

Charlie Palmer

Charlie Palmer, one of the most highly regarded chefs in the U.S. made his breakthrough in the New York dining scene in the 1980s, and has since established several prestigious restaurants in New York, California, and Las Vegas, including the Aureole at Mandalay Bay and the Charlie Palmer Steak at the Four Seasons.

City-Core Development, a real estate and investment-management company based in California, manages several mixed-use properties in the Western U.S. whose values collectively exceed $1.8 billion.

These two prominent forces have converged to create a unique non-gaming resort in Union Park, which will contain 426 rooms, with at least 100 of them as condo-hotel units. This project follows Palmer's previous plans for a $400 million condo-hotel on Tropicana Avenue, which fell through in early 2007.

The new project promises success as the first condo-hotel in the downtown area. The five-star resort will feature a 10,000-square-foot spa, a "Hollywood-style pool," and two five-star Charlie Palmer restaurants, without a single slot machine—a rare find among Las Vegas hotels.

Hint: *The condo-hotel units will be reasonably priced and will provide the first opportunity to own a piece of Union Park, the master plan development that promises to become an integral part of the core of Las Vegas. This is the first of several condo-hotels and fractional projects that will develop in the area.*

Pinnacle

The two towers of the Pinnacle condo-hotel project will be joined by a "sky bridge of four two-story townhomes suspended between the towers."

Pinnacle is located west of the Strip on Tropicana, across from the Orleans Hotel and Casino. The towers don't follow the usual block or L-shaped skyscraper design; instead, the Pinnacle towers are S-shaped (top looking down), gracing all units with unobstructed views.

Many of the project's amenities will be located on the roof of the six-story parking garage. In addition to the expected pools, the three-acre space will have a pet-friendly park, a jogging track, a snack bar, and even a "drive-in theater" for watching movies while in the pool or lounging on the pool deck.

The structure will cost $850 million, consisting of two 36-story towers with 1,104 residences featuring nine separate floor plans; the units will range from the mid 300,000s to $5 million. Completion is scheduled for the end of 2009.

Hint: *This has been a very ambitious project considering the current market and its location. The hotel management company is publicly traded and has a lot of experience in condo-hotel management. However, the project is located in an area that needs transition; warehouses and budget hotels currently surround the property.*

Fractional Ownership

While there are currently no fractional ownership properties available in Las Vegas besides La Scala at Lake Las Vegas Resort, you can expect to hear more about this real estate option in the near future.

Fractional ownership appeals to those seeking a second or third home but who don't want to pay for the property when they are not using it.

Fractional ownership usually involves impressive and expensive properties. Deeded shares are sold to a handful of owners, usually less than twelve; these owners have access to the property, and all the luxuries that come with it, for weeks at a time. The length of time is usually determined by the number of owners and how the shares are divided among them.

For example, if there are four owners who have equal shares, each would have access to the home for three months. Of course, the fewer owners there are, the higher the cost each pays and the more occupancy time each gets.

Fractional ownership allows for partial ownership of an upscale property by paying a fraction of the cost. To partially own a multi-million dollar property, the shares usually require an investment of $100,000 to $500,000. The properties can be anything from single-family houses to high-rise condos.

Fractional ownership is a variation of the timeshare and condo-hotel real estate concepts; however, it is very different for several reasons. Timeshares limit buyers to occupancy of a couple of weeks per year and are usually limited to less upscale properties; fractional ownership properties are usually larger and more luxurious, and offer access to amenities far beyond those of timeshare properties. There are also significantly fewer owners in a fractional situation, which means that owners have more access to the property.

In contrast, condo-hotels usually have a single owner who participates in a rental program; fractional owners usually do not rent the property during times of vacancy.

The fractional ownership trend has been fueled by Baby Boomers and retirees who are inclined to acquire multiple properties for pleasure, travel, and investment. Fractional ownership properties are ideal for those able to take extended vacations and who want five-star living.

Amenities at fractional ownership properties are often managed by companies with the highest standards and expectations, such as Ritz Carlton, Four Seasons, and Starwood Resorts. As a result, they have world-class comforts and access to spas, concierge service, private pools, and valet parking.

Fractionally owned properties are typically located in the most luxurious destinations, including Miami, Lake Tahoe, and Aspen. Because of the desirability of these locations, owners of fractional shares can easily sell their shares, and, thanks to appreciation, can usually profit from the sale. This is especially true when, as with condominium projects, there are incentives to purchase shares before construction begins. Committing early to a desirable project can result in significant investment gains.

Interestingly, the concept of fractional ownership comes from the business jet industry. Jet buyers, seeking to reduce the cost of owning a jet, realized that their jet often sat idle. By sharing ownership, not only were the costs spread among several parties, but the jets were used more effectively. The trend then moved to other luxury items such as sports cars and yachts. It was only a matter of time before developers began applying fractional ownership to luxury properties.

Fractional ownership is a real estate trend that will increase in popularity, especially among those interested in owning multiple homes in desirable locations throughout the world. Currently, there is only one property in the Lake Las Vegas Resort, but we can expect to see fractional ownership properties appear on the Las Vegas Strip in the near future. These properties will offer unique investment opportunities.

Chapter Seven
Investment Strategies

Choosing an Approach that Works for You

Initially, people overlooked the profit potential of investing in vertical residences simply because they themselves would not live in a building without a big yard and a private pool. These people disregarded the demand for such a product, especially in an entertainment center like Las Vegas. Nevertheless, the situation has changed.

As people move to Las Vegas from other metropolitan cities, they look for housing options that are familiar to them. In many cases, this includes a preference for the convenience of vertical living. These people want to avoid long commutes to work and like the convenience of living near entertainment and dining establishments.

Las Vegas also attracts people in the vacation-home market. The people in this category prefer high-rise, centrally located condos, because the residences are nearly care-free and are located near entertainment centers, such as the Strip.

When it comes to investing in the Las Vegas market, the usual methods for finding a good investment do not apply. In Las Vegas the vertical market is still rapidly expanding and constantly changing.

True, the residential housing market in Las Vegas has cooled since the days when houses were selling within hours of listing; however, the demand for vertical residences remains higher than supply. Entire buildings are selling out years before they are completed and, in many cases, before they have even broken ground.

The best profits in the Las Vegas real estate market have come from property value appreciation. A builder usually sells in "phases." As time goes on, builders release different sections of the project for sale. Each release is usually accompanied by a price increase, which can range anywhere from one to ten percent per phase, though the recent trend has been an increase of five percent or less each time a new phase is released.

This means that if you buy a condominium in "phase three" of a project that has six phases, your property may appreciate by about 15 percent by the time you close. Depending on how quickly the building is built, you could turn this profit in one to two years—a good return for a fairly stable investment.

As many people have found, investing in real estate is one of the safest and easiest ways to make money. You don't have to be a broker, an agent, or an investment expert to reserve a condominium unit, assuming you qualify and have the means. However, you do have to be knowledgeable and have patience.

Unlike the stock market, which fluctuates daily, the real estate market typically appreciates consistently with time. Even in slowdowns, as we are experiencing as I write this edition, properties continue to appreciate. The difference is that in the second phase of Manhattanizing, properties are no longer appreciating at 20 percent or more per year.

Besides focusing on appreciation, real estate investing offers a variety of options to generate additional income. Thus, besides providing a stable and consistent investment, the real estate market also offers investors options ranging from speculative flipping to conservative renting. Additionally, real estate investing offers a wonderful last-resort protection: if worse comes to worst, you can always live in your property.

In this chapter, I discuss options available to investors in vertical properties. These strategies are often different from more traditional real estate investment strategies, which focus on foreclosures and distressed properties that need to be fixed up. While these methods of investment are successful, they do not apply well to a new and emerging market like in Las Vegas.

What Type of Investor are You?

When it comes to investing in real estate, it is important to know what type of investor you are. This knowledge will help you understand what type of property you should look for, your tolerance for risk and your investment strategy.

Gary Keller, author of *The Millionaire Real Estate Investor*, says there are four types of investors:

observers, speculators, collectors, and prudent investors. Most people are observers, especially in the Las Vegas market. They watch the city grow and towers being built, and do not get involved in the expanding market. They are quick to discuss challenges such as rising interest rates and construction costs, but they miss investment opportunities, particularly in vertical living.

We have seen a lot of speculators in the Las Vegas real estate market, and the large number of their careless practices has caused some problems for the market. Speculators love the action of dynamic markets; they are the thrill-seekers of investing. Speculators seek quick profits, and as a result, they often buy projects that are not well-thought-through, resulting in the perception of a demand that may not be there.

Collectors buy for emotional reasons. Most of the marketing campaigns for vertical residences in Las Vegas have appealed to the emotions of potential buyers: we see grand buildings with spectacular views, interesting floor plans, and state-of-the-art furnishing, and we want it because it appeals to our hearts.

The potential of impressive appreciation also appeals to our emotions. When this occurs, we often fail to examine the facts and important factors, such as the experience of the developer and its team, and the strength of the financing.

When investing in real estate, you need to consider if there will be future buyers and renters for your unit. Just because you like a condominium project and would like to live in it yourself does not mean other people will have the same emotional response as you do.

Prudent investors take action while minimizing risks. Instead of buying for emotional reasons, they invest in value and stable projects. They study the market and learn about each project's strengths and weaknesses. Prudent investors consider the reputation of the developer and the construction company, and understand who the potential residents are and what their likes and dislikes are. Your goal should be to become a prudent investor.

The following are different strategies investors may have for their properties. Again, you should also consider the value of individual projects and the soundness of your strategy.

Flipping

When we talk about flipping these days, we are not speaking about the fraudulent practice of using a shill to manipulate a bank out of more money than the hidden price of the sale.

Flipping now refers to the practice of reserving a property soon after the building plan is announced to the public and then selling it before or soon after closing. In the case of vertical properties, the time between your initial reservation and closing could be 18 to 36 months.

Usually a buyer will be required to pay a deposit of five to ten percent of the purchase price when signing the contract. An additional five to ten percent will likely be required when the developer breaks ground and begins construction on the building. These deposit amounts are higher than traditional single-family residences; in fact, some projects may require up to 30 percent of the price by the time the reservation goes to contract. So, be aware that these higher down-payment percentages and the length of time it will take to complete the project will tie up your money for a longer period than a comparable investment in a traditional single-family house.

The advantage of such an investment is that the supply of available vertical residences has been lower than the demand. Currently, there are only a few projects that have actually been built; a person wanting to move into a vertical project now would have limited choices. This means that by the time you are ready to flip your property, it will be easier to find a buyer than if you were trying to flip a house in the suburbs.

Why wouldn't your future buyer simply do what you did? Your target buyer wants to move into the property right away, not wait years for it to be completed. He or she also wants to see and experience the property before purchasing it.

Example: *On November 29, 2004, I purchased a unit in the One Miami high-rise condominium building in Miami, Florida for $537,000. Over several months, I put a total of 20 percent down on the project, which was $107,400.*

That is a sizeable investment, but I had done my homework with the help of a local real estate broker Penni Chasens. This effort gave me confidence in the future demand for the building.

Less than a year later, on October 20, 2005, I sold the property for $700,000. That was a profit of $163,000 or a return of 151 percent on my initial investment in less than a year.

While an investment of more than $100,000 is significant by any standard, the return on the investment in such a short time period makes such an investment very attractive, despite being initially costly.

Additionally, the investment was a relatively safe one; even if I had not found a buyer, the property had already had a significant appreciation, so I could have sold the property at a discount and still made money on the venture.

Words of Warning: *While your return on investment for the property can be high, there are some risks for which you must be prepared.*

First, your money will be tied up for some time. Construction delays are common, so you cannot expect a return on investment within a specific time frame. Since resale programs (see below) are not widely available in Las Vegas, you are locked into your reservation for the length of time it takes to complete your unit.

Second, while rare, there have been times when developers have not increased the unit sales price on their properties as expected. While you can usually expect gains of about five percent for each phase of sales, developers are not required to make these increases. There may be market factors that require developers to slow or reduce appreciation in their projects.

Finally, you may not be able to find a buyer for your condominium when you close on the property. You need to be prepared and able to get a mortgage and close escrow, since it is unlikely that you will have a buyer lined up ready to purchase at the exact moment that you take possession of the property.

You will need to be able to finance and carry the property for the length of time it takes to find a buyer and sell your property. This could be a week, or it could be a few months or even a year. In the current Las Vegas market, you should have confidence that a buyer can be found within a reasonable time frame, but you still need to be aware of the risks.

Holding and Renting

Many investors, whether by choice or because they could not find a buyer to flip the property, hold their property and rent it. Instead of making automatic profit on the investment, holding and renting creates cash flow that will offer returns on your investment for years to come.

There are also financial reasons why a person might hold his or her property and rent it, even for a short-term monthly loss. Some people find it advantageous to show a monthly loss on their investments while they wait for their property to appreciate. This way, they can control when they show a profit on their investments.

Regardless of a person's reason for holding onto a property, vertical residences in Las Vegas are a good investment, especially if you are able to offer short-term rental periods. A property can generate a lot of money on a weekly basis in Las Vegas during big events such as New Years Eve and fight weekends.

However, before you choose this strategy, make sure you check the Covenants, Conditions and Restrictions (CC&Rs). Some properties limit the frequency of rentals to once a year. Technically, all rental applications should be submitted to the building manager and must be approved by the management hired by the Homeowners Association and its board of directors. This procedure allows the Homeowners Association to preserve the value of the property.

If you are interested in short-term rentals, condo-hotels are probably the best option for you. In the case of condo-hotels, the participating hotel will help you place short-term renters in your property. Of course, you can also stay at the property when you wish. Condo-hotels offer security for those interested in short-term rental investments.

Example: *I purchased a condominium on the South Strip in the first phase of sales. At the time, the unit price was $289,000. I only needed to put three percent down, or a total of $8,670 to acquire the property.*

I had an intuitive hunch, because of the relatively low down payment required and the people who had access to reservations early in the sales cycle, that many of the original buyers planned to flip their units. This meant that while the comparable price at closing was $450,000, there would be many people trying to sell their units all at once.

For this reason and some other factors, including the location of the project and the investment involved, I chose to rent the unit for a time, at least until the number of units on the market decreased and I could easily get my asking price for the condominium.

Holding and renting a condominium is a complicated investment strategy, but it will work for those investors who have certain portfolio needs and who have enough patience to put up with the occasional issues arising from short- or long-term tenants.

Investing with a Partner

Many people delay getting involved in the real estate market because they do not have enough money for sizable down payments. Even those with enough money to invest in large down payments may not want so much of their funds tied up in a single project.

For this reason, many sophisticated investors choose to partner with others to purchase properties. Since Nevada is a business-friendly state, it is relatively easy and inexpensive to set up a legal entity, such as an LLC, that formalizes the partnership so that you do not have to worry about misunderstandings between friends or associates. You can partner with any number of people; I have seen arrangements of up to ten investors on a single project.

As you can imagine, whether you are working with one person or several people, you want to make sure you have a signed agreement everyone understands. This agreement should state the group's investment goals and time-lines for the investment.

Example: *I partnered with a person on another unit at One Miami. I only had a 25-percent interest in the partnership, which meant that my contribution to a down payment for a $511,000 condominium was $22,550.*

When we sold the unit less than a year later for $669,000, my portion of the profits totaled $39,500. That is a 154-percent return on my investment.

Bold Offers

When it comes to investing in real estate, especially vertical properties, many people buy for emotional reasons months before a project is completed, but things change.

People may have enough money for a down payment, but for whatever reasons they may not be able to qualify for a mortgage for the project, or they may not be able to make payments on the mortgage and HOA monthly fees if they do not find a buyer or a renter.

As a careful investor, you have time on your side. If you are not emotionally involved in a property, you can afford to pass on the opportunity to purchase, knowing that other properties will soon be available.

In such cases, you have an opportunity to make bold offers on projects. Some might call this "low-balling." In defense of this concept, if a person is willing to sell for the "low" price offered, the buyer has found a good deal. Furthermore, the seller is able to get out of the property and probably still make money on their initial investment just before the opening.

The opening of a high-rise building is the perfect time to make bold offers. People with a flipping strategy often need to sell their unit quickly. With only 20 or 30 percent at risk, they only need to get their money back plus a little extra to come out ahead. This means that even if the unit has appreciated $100,000, and they are offered $50,000 more than the price they paid for the unit a year ago, they come out ahead and the buyer has an opportunity to purchase the property well below market price.

Example: *I made a series of bold offers on my current place of residence, Turnberry Place. I made seven offers on the property over a seven-month period.*

The previous owners of the last unit on which I made an offer complained that I was low-balling them; however, in the end we were able to agree on a price that was $300,000 below the appraisal for my acquisition loan for the condo. Not only did I get the *property for a low price, I also had the seller pay all closing costs.*

Resale Programs

In more established condominium markets like Miami, developers offer resale programs through which investors can assign their contracts once the building is completely sold and before it is completed.

During the development of a project, the sales office experiences occasional down-time. For instance, if a phase sells quickly, the sales associates have little else to do than to tell people when the next phase will begin selling.

Realizing that they have already paid the sales staff, many developers offer resale programs. In these programs, people who invested in an earlier phase can sell their unit before the building is completed.

The advantage for investors is that they are not required to keep their money tied up all the way to closing. If they choose, they can sell their reservation after only a few months and take their profits. This program also works for those who do not want to mortgage the property at closing while they wait for a buyer.

When you sell your contract, a realtor commission is usually paid to the sales office, and there are assignment fees that are shared by the developer with the sales staff involved in the transaction.

Usually, when you sell your contract, you will get your initial deposit refunded because the new owner-in-waiting replaces it with his or her own deposit. This means that your return on investment is the difference between your original contracted price and the price at which you sold your contract, minus commissions and assignment fees.

Although initially reluctant, many Las Vegas developers have come to recognize the value of resale programs.

Deposit Bonds

Deposit bonds are a relatively unknown financing alternative for real estate investors. While new to the United States, deposit bonds have been popular in other countries such as Australia and New Zealand for more than a decade.

A deposit bond acts as an alternative to cash for earnest deposits that are usually paid when you reserve a property. Deposit bonds work especially well during the early sales phases in high-rise projects. In such cases, buyers are asked to make down payments early in the development and construction process. In some cases, it may take years before you are able to close on the property, tying up your down payment for that whole time.

Deposit bonds can be used instead of cash when you make your down payment. You only pay small premiums for the deposit bond while the building is being built. At closing, you simply pay the property's full purchase price.

Many investors use equity from other properties to cover down payments. While this is an intelligent approach, it also comes with risks. Deposit bonds avoid these risks and allow you to keep your investments and savings active while you wait for the building to be built. Deposit bonds also cost less than other methods of financing.

A company I recommend, Deposit Alternative, has an underwriting agreement with OBE Specialty Insurance Company, one of the largest insurers and re-insurers. In this case, Deposit Alternative pays the property seller the amount of the deposit and OBE Insurance insures that you will pay the seller the full purchase price at closing. You, the buyer, sign an indemnity agreement when you receive the deposit bond.

Instead of seeking bridge financing or paying closing fees for loans, deposit bonds allow you to easily secure a down payment while your money continues to work for you. For instance, Deposit Alternatives can issue a deposit bond that represents a $60,000 deposit. You would pay approximately $2,700 plus applicable taxes and fees for the bond.

Alternatively, if you went with short-term financing for a $60,000 down payment, you would pay around $600 for an application fee, plus interest, which would be well over $4,000 over a year. In this example, the cost of a deposit bond would be at least half that of other types of financing.

Deposit bonds also offer you some protection if the developer doesn't break ground. In the case of Deposit

Alternative, the company will return the premium to you on a pro-rata basis with an administration fee.

In short, deposit bonds help you secure a property without tying up significant sums of money for months or even years. Or as Deposit Alternative CEO Louie Nehme says, "Deposit bonds truly accommodate and assist real people buying real property."

Options for Accredited Investors

An accredited investor is considered by the Securities and Exchange Commission (SEC) to be a person with a net worth exceeding $1 million, or a person whose individual income exceeded $200,000 in each of the last two years. If you match these qualifications and are considered accredited by the SEC, you are able to invest *with* developers as opposed to simply buying *from* them.

Many developers are searching for equity investors to participate in land acquisition, to share initial development costs, and to raise capital for the purpose of obtaining a construction loan. These investors participate in the profit of the whole project, not just the profit from the buying and selling of single units that are purchased from the sales office. By investing with a developer, accredited investors can gain significant returns on their investment once the project is completed and entirely sold.

There are many opportunities for accredited investors in vertical development in Las Vegas. If you qualify to participate in this type of investment, contact an appropriate real estate professional for the most lucrative investment opportunities available.

Chapter Eight
Choosing a Property

An 11-Step Strategy

It is just as important for an investor to study a property as it is for the developer to do due diligence before building a project.

1. Look at the surroundings. Marketers focus on what their properties offer, but in reality, we are concerned with what surrounds the property. Consider the neighborhood; check out what resources are available within walking distance. Where are the schools? How difficult will it be to purchase groceries?

2. Who is underwriting the project? Look at which bank is not only willing to finance the investment, but is also familiar with the type of real estate project being invested in. The more experienced the bank is, the more they will help the developer make educated decisions.

3. How experienced is the developer? You are investing a lot of money in the project—you need to have confidence in the developer's ability to

bring the project to completion. Look at what their past projects have been or the team they have assembled, and check how their sales in each phase went.

4. What is allowed in the governances? This is especially important for investors. There may be more stern rules in the governances that restrict what you can do with your property. For instance, the owner may not be able to rent out the unit, or they may be restricted by the length of time or the frequency with which they can rent the property (See Appendix C for a discussion of CC&Rs).

5. What services are offered at the property and what ensures that those services will persist? For instance, it is easy for a developer to say there will be a full-time concierge on a property, but what guarantees that a concierge will really be hired? Even if one is present when the project opens, will the position still be filled a year or two after construction is completed? Obviously, the owners may decide they do not want to pay for the concierge, but you should plan ahead and decide how important such a service is to you.

6. If the property is purchased after the construction is complete, investigate the Homeowners Association (HOA) as well as the members of the board. Board members are responsible for

many of the decisions that affect the value of your property. Periodically, HOA boards prepare financial reports and set budgets; consult these reports to make sure that the HOA is well-funded and is planning for future repairs and restoration.

7. If you are purchasing a property after construction is complete, you want to consider the record of the management company. The chart in Appendix B explains the different roles of the HOA and the management company.

8. Make sure the HOA is well insured. Liability insurance will protect the HOA and owners against personal injury lawsuits. The presence of a swimming pool and exercise facility present risks of such lawsuits. Also, property damage insurance will reimburse you and the HOA for damages that are caused by natural disasters and fire. While Las Vegas has not had a major earthquake in some time, fault lines in the valley make it possible.

9. Look to see if there have been lawsuits filed against the HOA or the developer. Lawsuits against the HOA may cost owners if a judgment is filed. If the developer is being sued for construction-related issues, a judgment could affect the appreciation of your property.

10. What is your comfort level with risk? Some projects are riskier than others; usually there are greater returns on riskier investments, but you need to decide how much risk you can handle.

11. Do you have the resources and credit rating to purchase the property when it becomes available? Even if you plan on flipping the property, you have to be ready to actually purchase the property if a buyer is not found quickly. If you plan on renting out the property, you also have to be prepared to cover your mortgage if you cannot find a renter right away.

There are many other important elements that will impact your decision, but the above steps are a good start. Consult real estate professionals and other members of your investment team to make sure you are making sound decisions.

CONCLUSION

As with any investment, there are certain risks associated with investing in vertical properties. Unlike other forms of investments, purchasing real estate for investment purposes ties up resources for a significant length of time. While waiting for a project to be built and then finding a buyer or renter for the property, any number of things can happen along the way. Anyone investing in real estate should be aware of these risks and how to mitigate them.

The Las Vegas real estate market remains dynamic and exciting. The addition of new vertical living to this mix has interested many investors who expect to experience sizable returns on their investments.

This market is developing so quickly that some of the information in this book will change by the time it is published. To remain current on this dynamic market, please contact me and request to be added to the update list to receive the latest information on vertical developments in Las Vegas and other real estate investment opportunities throughout the United States. You may also contact me to ask specific questions.

Whatever your participation may be in the next phase of growth in Las Vegas, it will certainly be exciting to watch the skyline change as new towers press upward.

APPENDICES

Appendix A

Las Vegas Statistics from *2007 Las Vegas Perspective*

Total Clark County Population in 2006: 1,912,654
Boulder City: 15,790
Henderson: 256,390
Las Vegas: 591,536
North Las Vegas: 202,520
Mesquite: 18,012
Unincorporated Rural: 31,357
Unincorporated Urban: 797,049

Newcomers in 2006: 96,057

Length of Residence	Own	Rent
Less than 1 year	2.4%	11.6%
1 to 5 years	20.7%	30.2%
6 to 10 years	18.6 %	17.4%
11 to 20 years	26.3%	19.8%
Over 20 years	32.0%	21.1%

Median New Home Price: $339,539
Median Resale Price: $286,542
New Homes Sold: 29,583
Resale Homes Sold: 41,892

Average Monthly Apartment Rental Rate:	$837.75
Median Household Income	$42,831
Under $20,000	11.0%
$20,000 - $24,999	11.4%
$25,000 - $34,999	14.9%
$35,000 - $49,999	23.1%
$50,000 - $74,999	25.3%
$75,000 - $99,999	8.4%
$100,000-$125,000	5.7%
Over $125,000	1.1%

(Source: *2007 Las Vegas Perspective*)

Appendix B

The Roles of the Homeowners' Association (HOA) and the Management Company

The HOA	The Management Company
Sets policies, rules, and regulations for the property	Implements the policies and enforces the rules and regulations set by the HOA
Approves the budget	Recommends a budget, then implements the budget after it is approved by the HOA
Authorizes pay level for employees of the property	Hires and supervises all employees of the property (maintenance, concierge, and other services) and recommends pay levels for each employee
Sets financial priorities	Authorizes expenditures based on the priorities set by the HOA
Approves expenditures	Pays invoices that have been approved by the HOA

The HOA	The Management Company
Receives owner complaints and passes them along to the management company	Resolves the complaints collected by the HOA or recommends an action to the board
Sets work priorities	Schedules work according to the priorities set by the HOA
Conducts board meetings	Recommends and prepares an agenda for board meetings
Establishes appropriate committees	Recommends the type, number, and purposes of committees
Approves written communications to owners	Following direction, creates communications between the board and owners
Approves all leases and resales	Contacts the owner or real estate agent's office and informs them of the board's decision.

Appendix C

Covenants, Conditions and Restrictions (CC&Rs)

The Covenants, Conditions and Restrictions (CC&Rs) can be a daunting document, but you should take the time to study what is in the document and make sure you are comfortable with what the homeowners' association will restrict.

Below, I outline the typical elements of CC&Rs and what you should look for in each section.

Board of Directors

Practically speaking, the board of directors is the executive, legislature, and judicial branches all in one. Check to see what recourse owners have when they feel the board has made an improper judgment or policy.

Amendment Process

The developer usually creates the first draft of bylaws, rules, and regulations for the HOA. Once the developer turns over operation of the association to the owners, the HOA can change any rule or procedure. You should understand the process for changing the HOA's policies and procedures, and be aware of such changes as they occur. A developer can promise many things that the HOA does not choose to provide.

Survey and Floor Plans

Make sure you understand what you own and what the HOA owns. Many people new to HOAs and condominiums fail to understand that they do not own their own front door or balconies. This means you cannot change the look and feel of your entrance or balcony, though it also protects you from suffering the negative effects of neighbors who want to dry their laundry outside.

Plan of Development

When you purchase a unit in the early phases of a development, make sure you know how the project will look when it is completed. You should know the number of units that will be available, the prices of future units and the amenities that will be offered in the future.

Percentage Ownership of Common Areas

Some HOAs distribute shares equally to owners, regardless of the sizes of their units. With other HOAs, ownership of common areas is passed on via the size and type of unit; this means that owners of larger units with a better position in the building may pay more for maintenance.

Parking

Parking is a significant issue in condominiums. With

limited available parking spots available, the HOA will set strict rules on who gets which spots and how to address visitor parking needs.

Easements

Easements are a common aspect of the CC&Rs, but you should understand that you will be using the elevator and hallways of the HOA to enter your unit. An easement is required to ensure that the HOA cannot simply post a no-trespassing sign and thus bar entry to your unit.

Common Expenses

Make sure you consult the common expenses section of the CC&Rs. Usually, this section is vague, giving the association a lot of flexibility when it comes to deciding expenses.

Association

Among many other things, this section of the CC&Rs usually gives the HOA board the right to enter any unit to make inspections and necessary repairs.

Voting Rights

Most HOAs use the "one unit, one vote" rule, though it is possible to extend more voting rights to owners who pay more for their units or own larger units, such as penthouses in a building that otherwise has less expensive and smaller units.

Amendments

Typically, the developer will have special rights when he or she controls the HOA. After the owners take over the HOA, amendments usually require a 75-percent vote to pass any amendments. However, your HOA may have different standards. You should also realize that mortgage lenders also have approval rights of amendments.

Sales, Transfer, Lease or Occupancy of a Unit

This section greatly restricts the uses of your unit. The HOA board must approve all leases and transfers. Such transfers may even include passing the unit onto your survivors in the event of your death.

Restraint upon Partition

This section of the CC&Rs prohibits people from selling memberships to the facilities in your building. It may seem obvious, but people have tried to sell access to pools and exercise facilities, especially when they do not use the facilities themselves.

Maintenance and Repairs

The Maintenance and Repairs section should clearly lay out what repairs the owner is responsible for and what maintenance the HOA will cover.

Use Restrictions

The Use Restrictions section may be particularly important for an investor. This section lays out how you may or may not use your property; for example, this section could prohibit home offices, or ensure that owners comply with health codes. Regulations may also limit the number of people living in a unit to prevent overcrowding in the building.

Insurance

Make sure the HOA has sufficient insurance and the proper type of insurance to protect not only the HOA, but you, from litigation.

Grills

Grills are generally a problem in Las Vegas for condominiums. Las Vegas fire code states that no open flame is permitted within 30 feet of a structure. Since most balconies are less than 30 feet from the building, charcoal and gas fires are generally not allowed.

Pets

While the rules on pets may not affect you personally, it could impact the sale or rental of your unit. Vertical properties have varying pet rules. Obviously, cats, and birds are easier to accommodate, but large dogs not only require more space, they also tend to bother other residents with their barking. However, few people will get rid of Fluffy just to rent or buy your condominium.

Flip Charges

There may be "flip charges" that apply to tenants moving in and out of a unit. The rationale assumes that people moving in and out tie up the elevator and do damage to the floor and walls of common areas.

Guests

There may be different rules applied to guests. In condominiums there is the issue of guest parking. There may also be rules concerning guest use of the pool and exercise areas, as well as limitations on how many guests an owner may invite to use these facilities.

Leases

An HOA could decide that no more leases will be allowed. Such an action would be rare, though there may come a time when the HOA wants a better mix of owner-occupied units in the building. Expect language in the leases section that makes the owner responsible for the behavior of your tenants and their guests.

Utility Services

In a condominium, the HOA may pay more utilities than one would expect for less densely-populated projects. One can expect the HOA to cover trash hauling, and they may cover other utilities as well.

Right of First Refusal

Usually an HOA will reserve the right to approve all buyers and tenants of your unit. Fortunately, if the HOA disapproves of a buyer or lessee, they must buy or lease your unit according to the same terms in your sales contract or lease agreement. This right allows the HOA to keep out undesirables without causing the owner economic difficulties.

Fines

Make sure you understand the nature and severity of fines. There have been incidents when fines accumulated to tens of thousands of dollars. Remember, the HOA can place a lien on your property should you fail to pay your fines.

Appendix D

Condo-Hotel Documents

Condo-hotel programs involve a lot of documentation. Below is a list of documents you can expect.

Association Documents
CC&Rs for the Association
Articles of Incorporation for the Association
Association Bylaws
Association Management Agreement

Resort Budget
Rules and Regulations for the Resort

Hotel Management Agreement
Pre-Opening Services Agreement
Marketing License Agreement
Operations License Agreement
Resort Service Agreement
Resort Access and Use Agreement

Pre-opening Agreement
Shared Facilities Covenant
Shared Facilities Rules and Regulations
Shared Facilities Budget

Purchase and Sale Agreement
Escrow Instructions
Purchaser's Acknowledgements
State Reports and Disclosures
Rental Program Agreement
Lists of Basic Services
List of Management Services
List of a la Carte Services
Reservation Agreement
Federal Truth-in-Lending Disclosure
Warranty Deed
Escrow Agreement

Appendix E

The Condo-Hotel Agreement

There are many different terms that may be addressed in your rental program agreement of which you should be aware:

Gross Rental Revenue

This is the total revenue that comes from the rentals themselves. It does not include revenues that come from other services such as charges for in-room movies, long distance calling fees, the sale of food and beverages, etc.

Net Rental Income

This is the Gross Rental Revenue less management fees, operation charges and payments to the FF&E reserve. Make sure you understand the amount and impact of each of these fees.

Operation Charges

Make sure these are defined and understood. Many can come under the category of operations:

- Commissions, fees, charges, and expenses paid to or incurred by third parties for the purposes of generating and collecting rental income

- Replacement costs for stolen or destroyed items, including sheets and towels
- Commissions paid to third parties for reservations, such as travel agents
- Credit card fees
- Loyalty reward program costs and redemptions
- Cost of maintaining a toll-free number for the travel industry
- Cost of creating and distributing marketing materials to travel agents
- Internet marketing costs
- Costs for accounting services

Furniture Fixtures and Equipment (FF&E) Reserve

All hotel rooms need to be refreshed from time to time. Couches need to be replaced, and occasionally a rock star may smash a television. The FF&E Reserve holds money in reserve for financing major upkeep.

Enrollment Fee

There will usually be a one-time fee for setting up the rental program.

Owner's Rental Proceeds

This is the percentage of the money you make from the rental program.

Owner's Operational Expenses

These are the expenses you are responsible for, such as the electricity, water, sewer, and cable TV charges. It also includes maintenance and repair charges.

Maintenance and Cleaning Costs

These costs will be subtracted from rental profits.

Emergency Repairs

Make sure you understand how emergency repairs are paid.

Deep Cleaning Costs

These costs are usually deducted from rental profits.

Hotel Services and Access Fee

Sometimes there will be fees for using the amenities of adjoining hotels or resorts. If the charges are not covered in the rental fee, you and your renters will need to pay these fees.

Entry of Unit

Usually the owner will be charged if the management needs to enter the unit for emergency repairs.

Acknowledgments

This book could not have been created without the invaluable input and assistance of many people.

Special thanks to Mayor Oscar Goodman for his inspiration and vision for the City of Las Vegas and its Manhattanization.

Thanks to the City of Las Vegas and the Office of Business Development for sharing their insights about the downtown redevelopment that is now well on its way.

I would like to thank the developers and their sales associates who agreed to be interviewed and who supplied information for this book.

Thanks to Richard Lee for inspiring my vision for this book and sharing insights into the high-rise market and real estate trends in Las Vegas.

Thanks to the Greater Las Vegas Association of REALTORS®, its Board of Directors, Executive Vice President Irene Vogel, and Government Affairs Director Kipp Cooper for their commitment and efforts to inform and educate real estate professionals about vertical living.

In addition to the insights provided by the development companies, I frequently relied on the local press as well as the Center for Business and Economic Research at the University of Nevada, Las Vegas - Dr. R. Keith Schwer. The *Las Vegas Review-Journal*, *Las Vegas Sun*, *Business Press*, and *In Business Las Vegas* were excellent resources. *Vegas Magazine* and *Las Vegas Perspective* provided helpful data.

Thanks to Brian Gordon and Jeremy Aguero of Applied Analysis for supplying the Las Vegas Valley Condo Maps throughout this book.

This book would not be a reality without the involvement of Jonathan Peters Ph.D., Karen McCalister, Cidney Dutton, and Rebecca Mostov.

Finally, I would like to thank those who read this book and recommended it to their friends and associates. I would also like to thank the real estate professionals who use this book as a tool to educate their clients. I wish you the best in your business and investments.

About the Author

Paul Murad is recognized as a leading authority on Las Vegas real estate and development. He is President of METROPLEX Group, a consortium of companies engaged in real estate brokerage, development, and investments. Paul holds a degree in Finance and International Business from the University of Tulsa. He has lived and worked across the globe, and is fluent in English, Russian, and Spanish.

Murad has been quoted by *New York Times Magazine*, the Associated Press, the Times Online (UK), *In Business Las Vegas, Las Vegas Review-Journal, Las Vegas Sun,* and *Las Vegas Business Press.* He has also been interviewed by Bloomberg Television, the Australian Broadcasting Corporation (ABC), as well as numerous local television and radio stations.

Prior to entering the real estate market, Murad owned several small businesses. He also worked in business development and finance for multinational corporations.

In his first year of real estate sales, Murad was selected by *REALTOR® Magazine* of the National

Association of REALTORS® as one of the top 30 young professionals in the nation.

In 2006, Murad was selected as one of the 40 Under 40 leading business people on the annual list published by *In Business Las Vegas*.

As a result of his real estate expertise, Murad is approved by the State of Nevada Real Estate Division to teach continuing education classes for real estate professionals and investors, including the popular High-Rise 101 course (see www.manhattanizing.com).

Murad is also a Broker for METROPLEX Realty, which offers full-service real estate brokerage services specializing in vertical properties, commercial real estate, development site acquisitions, and onsite project sales.

Murad is involved in many charitable organizations. He is a strong advocate of environmental initiatives, smart growth, and sustainable development.

For more information about the content of this book, development and investment opportunities, or speaking engagements, contact:

Paul@PaulMurad.com
702.450.2343 office

Notes

Printed in the United States
141318LV00002B/16/A

9 780976 953135

Notes

Printed in the United States
141318LV00002B/16/A

9 780976 953135